# RANDOM MEMORIES

# RANDOM MEMORIES

## Sam Raff

Aventine Press

Published by Aventine Press
1023 4th Ave #204
San Diego CA, 92101
www.aventinepress.com

ISBN: 1-59330-416-1

Printed in the United States of America

# To My Posterity

These stories are written in a random order so you won't miss anything by starting anyplace and stopping wherever you feel like. My purpose in preparing them is so that Gretchen, Lily, Nathan, Sara, Franklin, as well as even Terri, Nina, Melvin and others yet unborn can learn something about their families. Brian is already covered because he labored through it at the typewriter twice, corrected my spelling and grammar, and often re-arranged the sentences and even the stories. For me it's been fun and a labor of love.

# TABLE OF CONTENTS

# WHY I WORK

This story was told to me by my mother, but it's about my father. When he was a young man; before he was married, he was in merchandising, like so many Jewish immigrants of that period. Merchandising means he worked in a store. At one time my father worked for a man named Kresge. S.S. Kresge to be exact. At that time Kresge had two employees; my father and himself. One day he said to my father, "Nathan, I like you. You're a good worker and a smart young man, and I'd like you to work for me for a long, long time. Now what I'd like you to do is to take part of your salary in stock in this company. Think about it."

My father thought about it, and he consulted his father. My grandfather stroked his long gray beard and spoke the words, "Stock - my son?" As he shook his head from side to side with his eyes half closed.

And that is why I have to work for a living.

# POINT BARROW

I spent the early part of the winter of 1949-50 at Point Barrow, Alaska. Point Barrow is at the very north end of Alaska, sticking out into the Arctic Ocean. It is about as far north as you can go in North America, and at one time I remember being out at the edge of a little sand spit which stuck up to the north and being proud of the fact that I was the northernmost man in all of North America.

I think that one should visit Alaska in the winter, when it really is Alaska, and has all the distinctive features of what you would expect of the Arctic. Most people go up there in the summer. In the summer, Point Barrow is a bog, and it's full of great big mosquitoes that have spent the winter hibernating. It's what they call Tundra. It's quite flat because it's almost 500 miles north of the Brooks Range of mountains, and there are no mountains or even hills nearby. It's flat land that just runs right down to the beach. The temperature up there year-round is so low that the ground is frozen to the depth of about 700 feet. Only the top few feet thaw out in summer, when, of course, the sun shines all day and night and everything turns to slush.

In the winter, the ground is frozen fast, and, of course, the sun doesn't come up at all. When I arrived there it was past that time when the sun rose at Point Barrow. There were hours and hours of sunrise which loitered into sunset without the sun ever quite getting above the horizon. I remember I took pictures at noon there on the shortest day of the year, December 21st. I had double X film, which was the fastest film they had in those days. I took a number of different exposures to see which would come out better. I used a tripod, and the exposure that came out best was 6 seconds, but you can see. As a matter of fact, you can see all day and all night.

When I first arrived at Point Barrow, it wasn't very cold by Barrow standards. It was probably 8 degrees above zero, and ran up as high as freezing. But it was very, very windy. The wind was blowing about 40 knots, and that was the coldest I was up there. Later, when the temperature went to about 35 and 40 below zero, the air was still, and it didn't really get uncomfortable. As a matter of fact, I remember one night, we had been to the movie, and were walking back through the camp with our gloves off and our parka hoods down, and trying to guess the temperature. We were all kind of comfortable, but it was 35 degrees below zero.

We dressed very well. I brought long underwear with me, and when I arrived at the Arctic Research Laboratory, which was where I worked, they issued me some clothing, and included in it was long underwear. That underwear must have weighed about 5 lbs, and made the underwear I brought up seem like a silk chemise by comparison. We also got parkas with fur hoods, some long wool-lined pants and two pairs of boots. One pair was rubber and the other was leather. The problem with the rubber boots was that you perspire and after a while the socks get wet. Then you were terribly uncomfortable, so that late in the day your feet were cold, even indoors.

You couldn't spend very much time out of doors at a stretch anyhow, because the consumption of body heat was so great that you just got worn out. As a matter of fact, I don't think there was any period in my life when I ate as much as I did at Point Barrow. The local diet included a lot of ice cream. The fat content in it was believed to be good for keeping your body warm, and maybe it was.

We had a mess hall which was open all the time, day and night. They were serving breakfast and dinner at the same time because when people are in a climate with no day and night, they tend to go to sleep a little later each night. They get up a little later because it doesn't matter all that much. They have their own work to do; and they keep slipping a little and after a while they get completely out of step with the clock and after a little while longer they get back in step, but they've lost a day.

We slept in a big Quonset hut. There must have been about 50 beds in it, and most of them were occupied. Most of the time I was there, there was no time of the day or night when you could make noise or turn the bright lights on in the Quonset hut because someone was always sleeping. The Quonset hut had no plumbing because the ground was frozen so deep. Normally, they run the water and sewage 2 or 3 feet under the ground where it doesn't freeze in the winter. But with the ground being frozen to 700 feet, the only way you could run the water and sewage in the ground, particularly the sewage, was to heat it. That was quite a problem and they couldn't do that for the individual Quonset huts.

We therefore had the following bathroom arrangements. In the anterooms of each hut, at the ends, there was a line of old helmets. I guess they were from World War II. They had pipes welded to them, and the pipes went through the wall, outside the hut, and into barrels. If you had to pee, you just walked into that anteroom, which was moderately cold, and you stood up there and peed in one of the helmets. The problem was, that after a while the barrels would get full and frozen, the pipes would get full and frozen, and finally the helmets would get full and frozen. Then you would pee on this ice, and it would run over the edge of the helmet and drip on your feet. It seemed like this always happened when you had just gotten out of bed and were barefoot. Of course it was too dark to see clearly. You would be in this urgent situation, run out into the anteroom, find a helmet, and then all this iced water, or iced pee, came down on your bare feet and you couldn't stop. All you could do was try to shift your feet away from the splashing. It was a very unpleasant experience.

I remember my first trip to T-2. T-2 was the closest place where one could do major bathroom business. In fact, it was a 12 hole-er; 6 holes on a side, and there were barrels placed under the holes, the barrels being on the outside of the building and separated from the weather by a sort of plywood flap. On this first trip to T-2 I found that almost all of the holes on one side of the building were occupied and none of the holes on the other were occupied. Liking a little bit of privacy, though you couldn't get very much there, I sat down on the unoccupied side. I soon discovered why the holes on that side were unoccupied. That was the windward side of the building. It was the most extraordinary sensation. The worst problem was that after you were sitting there for a very brief time, your ass was numb, really numb, and you didn't know what was going on down there; you couldn't feel anything and you didn't know when you were finished. They tell me it can be worse. They say that the used toilet paper can come back up and hit you in the face.

During the time I was there, I saw them disposing of the metal barrels by simply hauling them out onto the Ice about 2 miles offshore. When the ice melted, the barrels would simply sink.

The Arctic Research Laboratory, where I lived during that period, was about 5 miles from the northern edge of the continent: right on the coast, almost on the beach. A little farther south along the coast, maybe 5 more miles, there was a bluff, where the land rises to a height of about 50 or 60 feet, and there was the Eskimo village of Barrow, which has been there a long time. There were a few hundred Eskimos in it. At that time they had a single gasoline driven generator which furnished electric power to the Eskimos, most of whom lived in wooden houses covered with tar papers. The charge was $5 per month per light bulb. They also had a big wooden church at Barrow, and I'll tell you more about that later.

Some of the people at The Arctic Research Lab were scientific types, but most of them were support people; cooks, bakers, and people to clean the place and level the snow at the airport. We had a little airfield up there. Most of the time I was there the whole place was covered with snow. They had a few hundred people at the lab. In addition to arctic research, it supported oil exploration. Some oil was coming in, and people were putting up drill rigs around the area. I never saw any of the rigs because they were not very close to the laboratory. They were about 30 miles out in various directions. They were looking for oil and doing various things that oil people do. That oil exploration was the basis for the north slope of Alaska oil which is now coming down through the big pipeline. At that time, however, the oil exploration didn't seem terribly important, and the most remarkable thing was the number of support people it took to keep one person doing useful work. It seemed like there were very few people working in the oil business up there, but an awful lot of people were there to support them in one way or another because it is so difficult to stay alive in the Arctic. I was told that drilling for oil cost about one dollar per foot in Texas and $100 per foot in the North Slope.

We traveled around in a small tracked vehicle called a Weasel. It was very good on the snow. It didn't go very fast, but you could get it up to about 20 mph if it wasn't too cold. It had tractor treads and lots of little cog-wheels, and when it was really cold, the grease would be so stiff that you could never get it out of low-low gear. But it was a very handy thing to have. The supplies were brought mainly by ship. They came in on the beach in September in landing craft. September was the time of the year when you could be most confident that there would be an ice-free beach. In the winter these supplies were carried to the outlying bases, primarily the oil exploration sites, on pipe sleds pulled in a train by huge tractors. I think they were called T-4s. I saw such a tractor pulling 10 pipe sleds, each loaded with 50 barrels of oil. The speed was a slow walk, and the operation could only be conducted in the winter when the ground and all the lakes were frozen hard.

While I was there I learned a little about the oil business in a one night a week volunteer course given by a geologist. They drill as deep as 4 miles and the soil pressure at that depth is about 10 - 20 thousand lbs per square inch. If they hit a pocket of oil or gas at that depth, the pressure forces it up the drill hole.

If it's gas, it can come up with a great rush and ignite and you have a well that's blown and all kinds of terrible problems. The way they prevent this is to keep the hole full of drill mud. That's a mixture of filler's earth and other stuff that has its density carefully adjusted to be the same as that of the surrounding earth so that the pressure is balanced and the gas or oil won't start up the drill hole. The mud is circulated down the hole at the center of the drill pipe and it comes up outside the pipe, between it and the casing, bringing up the drill chips.

When the ground is frozen, as it is at Barrow, you have to heat the drill mud to keep it from freezing in the well. When you do that, however, you thaw the ground around the well and the drill derrick is apt to shift. To prevent that you put pipes around the footing of the derrick and refrigerate the footings with cold oil. The only reasonable way to get cold oil to circulate around the footings is to cool it in the air — which they can only do in the winter. Therefore all drilling operations must be conducted in the winter. That's good because that's the only time they can transport materials anyhow. It's a complex business.

It was around Christmas time when I heard that there was going to be a dance at the Eskimo village 5 miles south of us. Nobody else wanted to go, so I took my Weasel and motored down and went to the dance. It was in the Eskimo church, which was a big heated building, and very warm. Now, it turns out that the Eskimos cure their fur by urinating on it and rolling it up in a ball. I gather that it's a pretty good process except for the residual smell. That is, the fur is cured just fine. It smells from urine, but in the cold, it's not too serious. On the other hand, when you get a whole bunch of Eskimos in a big, well-heated church, oh man! Fortunately your nostrils get accustomed to it after a while.

An Eskimo dance is like modern dance. A lot of people may be out on the floor, or one or two; however many are moved by the spirit. They dance individually. The dance tells a story. It's a kind of interpretive dancing. I recall that I was told by somebody there that one of their dances had something to do with Wiley

Post, who crashed around Point Barrow some time in the thirties. He landed in a lake and then took off and didn't have enough gas and crashed. However, I couldn't quite make that out from the motions the Eskimo was going through.

All this dancing is done to a band which consists of 4 or maybe 5 musicians. It's not music as we know it, but purely rhythm, beat out on Eskimo drums, which are nothing more than skin stretched out over a piece of whale bone which is bent into a circle. The night I was there, the spirit didn't move very many people to dance. There was one very old lady that seemed to be the mainstay of the dancing. When I asked somebody why they weren't dancing, they allowed as to how the musicians weren't very good. Of course I had no way of checking.

I stayed at the dance a while and then got in my Weasel and drove back up to the lab. When I got back, I put my Weasel in the garage, which one is supposed to do when the weather gets cold, and walked back the 4 blocks to my Quonset hut. As I was walking I heard a very strange sound. There was something eerie about it. At first I thought there was a dog following me and crunching the snow. There were lots of dogs up there; too many. Once in a while they'd have a dog shoot and kill a whole bunch of them. That night I turned around and looked, but couldn't see a dog crunching in the snow. Presently I decided that it must be connected with something someone had told me about the ice moving on the beach. I headed toward the beach, and sure enough, there was the ice coming up the beach, a very strange phenomenon which apparently last happened there in 1917. It's a loud intermittent creaking sound. The process happens when the sea freezes and the wind blows across a huge sheet of ice. It may be blowing in the same direction for hundreds of miles, over thousands, and maybe ten thousands of square miles of ice. Although the force on any particular small area of ice is not very large, when you add up those forces over very large distances, something has to give at the end.

This is the reason there is what they call floe-ice in the Arctic. You have this big sheet of ice, and the wind is blowing in slightly different directions in different areas. At one point the wind may be blowing toward the east, and a few hundred miles away, it may be blowing toward the west. The wind is pushing the ice and either it is going to open up cracks in the ice or it is going to compress the ice and push it together. When it compresses the ice, you get a line where the ice cracks and begins to fold and pile up on top of itself. Then what's called a pressure ridge develops. A pressure ridge may run for hundreds of miles; a curvy, wiggly line where there is a pile of ice. Most pressure ridge piles of ice are massive. They may be 50, 60 feet high before the ice stops crunching together. They are so massive that in the spring when the thin ice around them melts, those pressure ridges don't melt. They stay and drift around all summer. It's called pack ice or floe ice.

The normal process at Point Barrow is that in the fall, the wind and currents in the Arctic are such that some of this old floe ice, which is there from the last winter, comes ashore on a sand bar a few miles off the coast and is massive enough to act like an anchor for the fresh frozen ice. Then when the wind blows toward shore on this fresh (young) ice, the anchor holds it and the young ice will crack against this grounded floe ice.

The particular year I was at Point Barrow, I knew, from the informal courses we were taking, that the floe ice had not come close to us and run aground. There wasn't any floe ice on that sand bar where it had come ashore every year since 1917. Therefore, when the young ice froze, it froze directly out from the beach all the way out into the Arctic. What happened that night, around Christmas time, was that there had been an on-shore wind for several days. All the leads were closed up, and the ice was being pushed up against shore, and it was starting to move up the beach. The sound was very strange, a lot of short creaks, then a pause, then a lot of short creaks. What makes the sound so eerie is that the ice is moving as a unit and the creaking sounds are in synchronism all along the beach. Therefore the sound doesn't come from just one place. We're not used to hearing sounds that don't come from a particular point, and it has a funny effect on your ears and your hearing. You can't tell where the sound is coming from. I guess that's why I thought there must be a dog following behind me when I first heard it.

The ice was moving up the beach just a few feet a minute, not very fast at all. I found it exciting, so I quickly walked back the few blocks to the Quonset hut and told some of the guys that the ice was coming up the beach: that it was a rare sight, and one ought to come and see it. But everybody looked sort of asleep, or not very anxious to go out in the cold. Two of the guys did come down to the beach and they saw it. Then they went back to rouse the rest of the guys. Then everybody came down, but by then the ice had stopped moving.

They measured afterwards that the ice had moved a distance of 176 feet. The only thing that stopped it was that it began to crumble on its leading edge, and after a while there was a big pile of ice on the beach which was quite heavy. That began to anchor the young ice and then it broke farther back. But when it stopped moving, there was a huge pile of blocks of ice; most of them about 3 feet thick, and some of them about 15 feet long and 10 feet across. They were slanted at funny angles, stuck on top of each other, and the leading edge of that pile of ice was so close to the cook shack that there was just enough room to squeeze through between it and the shack. If it had moved just another 3 feet, it would have knocked the shack down. Afterwards they mounted an ice watch. They always had somebody on the beach so that if the ice started to move they could alert the camp and we could move out. Though exactly where we would move, or what we would do in that extremely inhospitable area I have no idea. Maybe we'd have just moved to the huts that were farthest from the beach.

The reason I had some idea to expect the ice movement was because we had set up two informal courses, each one night a week. The purpose was to educate ourselves a little bit, or educate each other, as well as to pass the time. There wasn't very much to do up there. There was a movie every night, and a poker game that I'll tell you about later. You were allowed 5 cans of beer and 5 cokes a week. Hard liquor was absolutely forbidden, although everybody that came in brought some.

One of these informal courses was given by Dr. Radar Wenesland, who was a medical doctor doing research. He had come up there to study the metabolism of the Arctic Codfish. The Codfish travels with and lives under the Arctic floe ice. The polar bears travel with the floe ice too because they eat the Codfish. By the way, the interesting thing about the metabolism of the Arctic Codfish is that they can get frozen into the ice in the winter and survive. One of the reasons Dr. Wenesland was giving this course was because he hadn't any codfish to study. The currents that normally bring the pack ice, the Codfish and the polar bears into the Point Barrow region were missing that year, so that's how I knew that the pack ice had not been grounded on that sandbar.

The other course was on Geology, and had to do mostly with oil, how one drills for it, geosynclines, what kind of formations you find oil in, and how you drill for it, and that kind of thing. I can't remember the name of the instructor. He was a geologist, and he also talked about the motion of the ice, and the formation of leads, and so on. Putting these things together, the thought had crossed my mind that the ice might be coming up on the beach, and so when it actually happened that night, I was prepared for it, and dashed down and saw it. Later I took some pictures of the pile of ice. I have them someplace. They were taken with that long, long exposure, the double X film, and of course it was in black and white. In those days, color film was pretty scarce and not very fast. Except for the scientists, most of the people who worked at Barrow were support people and not very skilled; although some were bakers and cooks. They signed up for two years and they would get a vacation after one year. During their vacation the lab would pay their airfare back to Fairbanks, which was, by Barrow standards, high civilization. As you might expect, most of these people who signed up for 2 years were social outcasts in one way or another; although there were a few who were really up there to make their stake in society; to save the money to start a business. They could certainly do that because, although the wages weren't high, they worked 9 hours a day, seven days a week, and got paid time and a half for 23 hours. Room and board cost about $3 a week; cokes and beers cost a nickel each, and the movies cost a dime; so there wasn't any way to spend money. You could accumulate dollars if you wanted to, but most of the support people up there had unhappy marriages, were escaping from one thing or another, or just hated people, and weren't interested in making a stake. They came to get away from the world. They would sign up again after their two years were up, have a brief trip to The States and then come on up again.

Well, as you might suppose, for those people, the money didn't really mean very much. They had no way to spend it except for taking a vacation in Fairbanks. As a matter of fact, the story is told that one of them spent a week in Fairbanks during which he not only bought drinks for everybody in every bar he walked into, but he hired a taxi by the week and had the cab driver following him around all the time.

Among these support people there was a poker game; a friendly sort of a game that went on every night and quit early so they could all get their rest. The game was played among the social outcast types. My acquaintance with the poker game was completely hearsay until one evening about 10 o'clock I was in the mess hall having a cup of coffee and a piece of cake before going to bed. I was sitting at a long table and sitting directly across from me somebody was counting bills. He had a stack of fives and a stack of tens and a stack of twenties; big stacks like you'd expect a bank to have, almost ready to fall over. So I said to him, kind of as a joke, "How'd you make out at the poker game tonight?"

"Well, Joe over there was the big winner," he answered.

There are lots of stories about that poker game, including one about a guy that got in the game and didn't play like everybody else. He played to make money. He didn't take too many chances, only bet when he had a good hand, no bluffing. He was really serious about making money, and he did, but after 2 nights they threw him out of the game because they said, "You know, you're going to walk off with all the money in the game unless we all play your way, and if we play your way, it won't be very much fun."

From the day I arrived up there to the day I left, the ground was covered with snow. When the wind blew, it blew dry, fine powdery snow. You never could tell whether it was snowing or not because whenever the wind blew, there was snow in the air, and it was higher than your head. I suppose that at some height, if it wasn't actually snowing, the air would be clear, but you never got to that height. The snow was so fine that the laboratory had a problem of what to do with the Quonset huts that were not in use. The logical thing to do, of course, was to seal them up and not heat them and just leave them alone. Unfortunately, there were keyholes at both ends of the hut, and when this fine powdery snow blew, some of it would blow in the keyhole. Once it got inside the hut, of course, the air wasn't moving very much, and it would settle out. It would settle out against the door under the keyhole. Presently there would be a very significant amount of snow there. The doors opened in, and by the time the snow piled up to the keyhole, you couldn't open the door. That is one of the strange problems that people have up in the Arctic and have to find solutions for. I think the solution they ultimately found was to tape the keyholes and nil the cracks around the doors.

Another problem which we had in the Quonset hut was that we had no thermostat. We had an oil stove in the middle of the hut, or maybe there were two of them. You could set the rate of burning in them, but the problem was that the temperature differential between inside and outside was so large that there was no way to maintain a constant comfortable temperature inside except to pay continuous attention to the flame. If it was too cold, you had to turn the flame up and vice versa. Sometimes when everybody in the hut was asleep, the wind would change. If the wind died down, the temperature in the hut could go up to over 90°; and the air was incredibly dry. You would wake up just dried out like a prune, and your throat would hurt. If the wind increased during the night the temperature in the hut would go down, and that was one of the important uses of the bottles of coke. You'd put them on the floor next to your bed, and before you got out of bed you'd look at the coke bottles. If they were frozen, and you were that kind of guy, you'd stay in bed until someone else turned the stove up.

My research at Point Barrow consisted of 2 things that I intended to do, one of which was to measure the variations in the earth's magnetic field. You know the magnetic field of the earth is not really steady. There are fluctuations, like pulsations and micro pulsations, and things like that. They have periods of about 1 second to 6 minutes, and there is a lot of character to the variation in the earth's magnetic field. My objective was to try to correlate some of these fluctuations with the Northern Lights (the Aurora Borealis). For that purpose I intended to put down a big coil of wire on the ground way up at the north end of that sand spit I talked about. It was very far from any power lines and other man made things that would produce currents in it. I intended to measure the currents in that coil of wire. I had a big drum of wire shipped up there, the kind that the power companies use. It had about 1/2 mile of seven-conductor wire on it, and I intended to hook it up in a coil. We had a building up there were we worked, and we had a thing called a wannigan, which was a little hut about 4' x 6' with runners under it. We hauled the wannigan out to the end of the sand spit and connected it to a small makeshift wire coil because the coil we ordered didn't show up for some reason.

The instrumentation we had included a chart recorder in the wannigan which we could run at different speeds. The chart recorder shared the wannigan with a stove, leaving us Just enough room to walk around inside. We had a 5 kilowatt electric generator that powered our equipment, but I'll tell you more about that later.

The laboratory we had was back at The Arctic Research Laboratory proper. It was just a little bit bigger than the wannigan, but it was hard to get to because there was a big pile of snow right in front of the door. To go in or out the door, you had to squeeze around this huge pile of snow. It was serviceable though, and we had some equipment there. We got some interesting results and correlations. The Aurora Borealis was really pretty. The Northern Lights as seen from Barrow are to the south, for some reason having to do with the earth's magnetic field and its orientation. They were indeed very spectacular some nights, moving multi-colored curtains of light. The magnetic field appeared to vary more when the Aurora Borealis was visible, but we could not be conclusive because of equipment problems.

As I mentioned, we looked all over for the big coil of seven-conductor wire. We sent telegrams to Seattle where it was supposed to come from, to the resident officer in charge of construction, who was ROINC, a very important guy, and they traced that coil all over. As near as anyone could tell it had gone through Seattle. The records weren't very good.

We also had a lot of problems with the electric generator. I guess the first thing that happened was that every time we had to shut it down to check the oil, it was almost impossible to start up again. To start something in the Arctic when it is very cold (airplanes too cool down when they've been standing outside), you have two very important tools. One of them is the gasoline blow-torch which you can light under any conditions whatsoever. The other is what's called a Herman-Nelson. A Herman Nelson is a gasoline burner, a fan driven by a small lawnmower-type gas engine and a canvass funnel. It sucks in the cold air and blows it onto the gasoline flame, which warms it up and then it blows the warm air on whatever you put the canvass funnel on. They heat up airplane and automobile engines that way, for example. The blowtorch is used to start the Herman-Nelson.

When we shut down our gasoline generator to check the oil, it never got very cold because it wasn't shut down long enough. When we started it up again, which we did with a crank, it would fire a little bit and then absolutely quit. You would crank it until you were completely exhausted and nothing would happen. Finally you would start to check out what was wrong with it and you'd take the spark plugs out, which was the first thing to do with an engine that won't run in the Arctic. We'd check them and re-gap them a little bit, horse around with the motor generally, and then put them all back together and then it would start.

After a while we recognized this pattern. It was consistent. It would fire a little bit. It would quit. And then absolutely nothing would happen until we checked out all the plugs and re-gapped them. Then it would start. Finally John Huff, who was the Chief Machinist at The Arctic Research Laboratory, and a veritable storehouse of knowledge, information and skill, explained this all to us. When we shut down the engine, it would start to cool. Because the engine itself was very massive but the spark plugs were thermally insulated from the rest of the engine, they would cool first. Therefore, when you'd start the engine, the coldest point inside the cylinder was the spark plug. When the engine fired, the products of combustion include a lot of water, which would condense right across the gap of the spark plug. The spark plug, therefore, couldn't fire again. When we took the plugs out and fooled around with them, without being specifically aware of it, we wiped or shook the water off the gap. Meanwhile the engine was cooling, and by the time we finished horsing around and put it all back together, there wasn't that much thermal differential between the spark plug and the rest of the cylinder, and therefore the products of combustion would not condense selectively on the spark plug gap and the engine would run.

It was a marvelously simple phenomenon once you understood it, and the solution was similarly interesting. After you stopped the engine and checked the oil, you lit a blow torch, took the wires off the spark plugs, and played the blow torch on the spark plugs for a few minutes to warm them up. Then you could start the engine.

That's what we did, and after that we never had any trouble. Except, one day, the snow started blowing, and this gasoline engine wasn't in the wannigan; there wasn't room for it. It was on another sled, on the outside and completely exposed to the elements. The generator consists of three units on the same shaft. There's the gasoline engine on one end; next there is an electric generator, and then a little exciter at the other end. The exciter is a small D.C. generator that generates the voltage for its own electric field as well as for the field of the main generator. In order to cool all this in normal operation, there's some fan action which sucks air in over the generator and then blows it over the exciter and then out. When the snow started to blow, it got sucked in by the fan action, blew across the generator and then across the exciter. Now the exciter has a commutator with brushes that ride on it. The snow melted going over the generator, and when it got to the exciter, which was somewhat cooler, it began to condense and freeze again. It formed a layer of ice over the commutator.

The brushes then ride on this layer of ice and there's no contact. Therefore there's no electric field generated.

When we came out after the snow blow, everything was running. That is, the gasoline engine was running, it was turning the generator over, it was turning the exciter; but there was no voltage because the exciter commutator was not being contacted and therefore no voltage was being generated for the field. To make the thing worse, because the exciter was running in the earth's magnetic field and was turning over and over and over, not generating any voltage, the residual magnetism in it disappeared. It de-permed itself.

After we hauled the generator back to the laboratory on the sled and got it running in the lab and got all the ice off of it, we still couldn't get any voltage because it takes a little residual magnetism in the exciter to get the whole thing started. We didn't have any left. Boy, it took a long time to figure that one out.

After some consultation with John Huff, we decided the thing to do the next time the snow blew was just to shut the whole thing down immediately. We did that the next time, and that turned out to be an even worse disaster. The blowing snow worked its way into all the cracks in the generator and the motor and melted and refroze into ice, and the whole generator was now packed in ice and there was no way you could turn it over. As a matter of fact, we brought it back into the main shop on the sled and set it down a few feet away from a roaring oil stove and left it there for about a day. Finally we could turn it over by jumping on the crank.

The ultimate solution to the generator problem was that we built a little wood frame and put a tent around the generator. That stopped the snow from blowing against it, and then we could keep it operating when the snow blew.

The next problem we had was that the generator, after a while, simply wore out. Apparently it was a small generator, and it was heavily loaded, and it was designed to be used only intermittently in case of power failure. By running it continuously like that, we simply used it up. We had to put new pistons in it. Those were hard to get. We finally got them though, and we got the generator running again. Bye and large, it gave us reasonable service during most of the time we were up there.

The other scientific work that I had planned to do while I was up there was to measure the radio frequency electrical properties of sea ice. For this purpose I brought along some high frequency impedance measuring equipment; signal generators, wheatstone bridges, and things of that type. I had the intention of putting the ice between the plates of a capacitor and measuring its dielectric properties, or conducting properties, or whatever. That turned out to be an absolute fiasco. The electrical properties of sea ice are completely baffling. It seemed like there was no way I could ever get the same measurement twice. It was exasperating, and I afterwards discovered that it is reasonably known that the properties of sea ice are governed by small filaments of salty ice water that are in the ice. These filaments wiggle, move, squiggle and they are directional. I think to this day people don't know much about the electrical properties of sea ice.

With all the electrical equipment we had though, at one point we were picking up a signal from a ham operator down the street at The Arctic Research Laboratory. We broadcast a very weak signal back to him from the signal generator, voice modulated it, and pretended we were in Australia. He got a real big thrill out of that, and went around telling everybody how through some fluke in the atmospheric phenomena he had made contact with a radio ham in Australia. We let him in on it after a while.

No story of Point Barrow in the winter time would be complete without some discussion of the phenomenon called white-out. This is a very strange thing. The ground is covered with snow. It's fairly uniform and flat, and when the sky is overcast, the ground and the sky blend together in such a way that you can't find the horizon. Now the visibility is good under white-out conditions: that is, you can actually see. There's no fog or anything like that. There's no snow blowing. Because you can't find the horizon, however, very strange tricks are played on your mind and on your vision. You see very much by shadows, and when the sky is overcast and the ground is perfectly reflecting like that, the light is very diffuse. It's coming from all directions after bouncing from the overcast sky to the snow covered ground and back and forth. The shadows are missing, and because there's also no horizon, all your visual judgment seems to be gone. Your depth perception is completely destroyed. You're used to deciding how far away things are by their relationship to the horizon, and there's no horizon. You can't tell whether you're looking at a small object that's close to you or a large object which is far away. Flying is pretty much out of the question, and in some cases, it is even pretty difficult to walk. That is, if the ground is not really flat, you can misjudge whether the ground in front of you is sloping up or down, and you can step into a depression without even seeing it.

One thing I learned while I was up there was great respect for the intelligence of the Eskimos. Of course, they are magnificent in their own environment and habitat. When the snow is blowing, for example, you're quickly completely lost, whether your walking, or driving a Weasel; you don't know which way is home; you don't know anything. In fact, you must not make a trip into any unfamiliar territory even 2 or 3 miles from the lab, even with a Weasel, without an Eskimo along. The Eskimos always keep their sense of direction, and furthermore, they know what the weather is all about and what's going to happen.

I recall on one occasion I was away from the base with an Eskimo named Hoover. I guess that gives you some idea of when he was born, probably named after Herbert Hoover. The snow was blowing. The weather was absolutely miserable. There was scarcely enough light to see anything by. In addition, it was overcast. I remember his remark, "Gonna be pretty nice pretty soon."

I thought he was crazy. But about half an hour later, the wind died and the air was still. The sky was clear, and the weather was lovely.

That, you expect from them, but what was surprising was their incredible aptitude with machinery. We were out on the ice one time, taking samples, and the intention was to drill a hole through the ice. We had 3 hand drills, and one of them was a left-handed drill; it went the other way. It always confused me. Hoover had never done this sort of thing before. I drilled the 1st hole, and then I handed him the other drill, the one that was left-handed. He looked at it and turned it left-handed immediately. No question! Then John Huff told me that the Eskimos are excellent machinery operators; cranes and tractors and things like that. He said that they also learn to run a lathe considerably faster than the average American.

The Eskimos are, however, very easy going people, and very susceptible to alcohol. As I understand it, their normal diet consists completely of meat and fish. There are no vegetables, no fruit and no grains. There is nothing in their natural diet that can be fermented. Therefore they have no alcohol, historically, of any type; no wines, no beer, no nothing. When they start to drink, they have absolutely no control, and it can turn into a disaster. There was a story up in Barrow about when in the early days, somebody brought up a barrel of flour and fermented it and made some kind of drink and gave it to the Eskimos. They had a roaring drunk. There was a lot of fighting and a lot of people dead in the village before it was over. So it has always been a rule in The Arctic Research Laboratory that anybody that gives alcohol to an Eskimo is sent home on the next plane. Furthermore, no alcohol is supposed to be brought up there, although that's a rule that is widely violated. Most of the people that go down to Fairbanks for their vacation, or that come up from the states on their 2nd trip, whether they're support people or laboratory personnel, are expected to bring up hard liquor in their luggage. Their luggage is handled very gently. Anything they need in the way of clothing, they can use to wrap the liquor bottles, or they can buy it up there. As a matter of fact, the people that met me at the airport were very disappointed that I didn't have any, but I didn't know anything about it.

It took me a while to learn about the Eskimos. Frankly, I had misunderstood them, and one of the things that I misunderstood was why there was a rule at The Arctic Research Laboratory that when the hunting season starts, any Eskimo who leaves his job to go hunting will be summarily fired. I always interpreted that as part of their happy-go-lucky character and the fact that they were hunters by nature. In fact, in Barrow the hunting season begins when the floe ice comes in, because that's when the polar bears come in with the seals and the Arctic Codfish.

I later learned, before I left, what this hunting was all about. It's a big business, and the Eskimos can make more money hunting in 3 or 4 weeks at the beginning of the season than they can working at The Arctic Research Laboratory for the whole year. They are, or were then, wards of the U.S. Government, and they were the only ones allowed to hunt commercially. The pelts are worth a lot of money. They hunt with rifles, of course, and they do very well. In fact, about the time I left, they were instituting a suit against Pan Am because there were 15 Eskimos who had contracted with Pan Am to fly them up to some place where they thought the hunting would be particularly good, and the Pan Am plane was 2 weeks late. They claimed that they had lost an enormous amount of money by not starting their hunting season on time. That's a far cry from my initial picture of these happy-go-lucky aborigines who, because of some quirk in their inner nature, couldn't resist going out to hunt at the beginning of the season.

Along similar lines is the story of my attempt to buy one of these little skin and whale bone drums that they use in their musical bands. I thought it would be a wonderful souvenir of Alaska. I couldn't get one, but someone at the lab arranged for one of the Eskimos to make one for me. It wasn't ready when I left, so I received it in the mail about a month after I got home. It had come apart in the shipping. It was a pretty cruddy looking thing, and in with it was a bill for $40, which in those days was almost as much money as I made in a week. I recall rewrapping it, sending it back to Alaska, and telling them to forget it. I guess the moral is that the Eskimos have pretty good commercial instincts.

When I came back rather late in the winter, they asked me to accompany an Eskimo boy who had broken his arm and was being sent back to a hospital in Fairbanks to make sure that it was set right. This was a very quiet and very frightened boy. Not only did he have the pain of a broken arm, but I don't think he'd ever been more than 5 or 6 miles from home before in his life, and here he was in an airplane, sitting next to a total stranger, going to someplace he had only heard about in the wildest stories, to a hospital. He was scared and he was shy and he was quiet. We sat side by side in that airplane and I tried to engage him in conversation and pleasantries. He spoke English because he had been to the schools up in Barrow, but I could hardly get anything out of him but grunts. He didn't eat anything they served to him on the plane, and I felt terribly sorry for him, but there wasn't much I could do. My job was, when we got to Fairbanks, to make sure that he got to the hospital; I had directions and instructions. Well, it was all superfluous because the government took very good care of him. When we arrived at the airport there was someone to meet him with a car and take him directly to the hospital. I went along more for the experience than because I was needed. The kid said absolutely nothing, and when he arrived at the hospital he was greeted by a young Eskimo on crutches who looked like he was about 20. The kid was about 8. It turned out that this young Eskimo on crutches was an uncle of his who had been sent down a week or two before with a broken leg. Boy! Were they happy to see each other. I never understood about Eskimos rubbing noses, but the boy and his uncle stood together with their faces close to each other and their noses touching, and the tears ran down on the floor between them. I don't know who was crying; probably both of them.

The next day, when he had had his arm checked I came back to see him. I brought him some toy in a little paper bag. He was in his bed asleep. He didn't move and I didn't wake him. I sat a few minutes, and then I left the bag on the bed and walked away. I got a few steps away from the door, turned around and came back quietly, and there he was with the bag open and the toys out. He obviously hadn't been sleeping. He was a very shy kid.

I mentioned the Eskimo church in connection with the dance. It was a Christian church. The Eskimos had been converted, with a modicum of confusion. On the way to the sand spit where we had our coil and wannigan was a single tarpaper shack all alone by itself. An Eskimo with two wives lived there. The Christian community wouldn't let him live in the village because monogamy was a tenet of their faith. But what was he supposed to do with his other wife? Put her out in the cold to starve to death?

Another point of conflict between the new civilization and the old Eskimo culture related to suicide. In the olden times, when an Eskimo was old and useless, it was common to commit suicide and fairly usual for his children to help him at it if they could thereby make his demise less painful. I heard a story about an Eskimo who helped his old mother hang herself. To the local administration that was murder, and he was tried and sentenced to a year in jail. The bright side of the picture, however, was that he thought the jail was a pretty good deal. He was warm and well fed and compared to the rigors of his normal Arctic life, it was okay.

I left Point Barrow and came home in late January. Lillian was big with Brian, and Melvin completely rejected me for the first hour or so because I had grown a moustache, and I guess he didn't recognize me. The scientific experiments were carried on by another team from NOL after that, and they found the reel of seven-conductor cable. When the snow melted they discovered that it was the base and principal substance of the pile of snow in front of our lab that we had been squeezing past all winter.

# MY FAVORITE QUOTES

MAURICE CHEVALIER
Growing old is not so bad -- when you consider the alternatives

GEORGE BURNS
My idea of outdoor exercise is smoking a cigar with the window open.

DWIGHT D. EISENHOWER - on the golf course.
God give me strength to hit this ball easy.

ME
The difference between the good guys and the bad guys is not just that we're the good guys, but the bad guys can't get along with each other.

KING SOLOMON
The race is not always to the swift nor the battle to the strong, but time, and chance pay their part.

ANNA BUCKNER - on the same subject.
You gotta have mozel.

GROUCHO MARX
I wouldn't join a country club that takes members like me.

BOB FROSCH'S UNCLE
I have a penny that predicts presidential elections. Heads, it's Republican, tails Democratic. It's been right every time since 1920. I got it by starting with 200 pennies -- I think this applies to advertised mutual funds.

MILTON KRONHEIM
When you get old three things happen to you. One is that you begin to lose your memory. The other two I forget.

FANNIE RAFF
It's just as easy to fall in love with a rich boy.

IZZY ADLER
Fitness after fifty is learning to live with pain.

MARK TWAIN
The God of the Old Testament and the God of The New Testament is really the same God, but the Old Testament was before he got religion

FANNIE RAFF
If you eat spinach for 60 years, you'll live a long time.

NATHAN RAFF (the elder)
You change their diapers and go to school to argue with their teachers, and one day you find they are other people you can get along with if you're careful.

MEL RAFF
I used to be conceited, but now I'm perfect. (said in jest)

EDDIE RAFF
God hates a coward.

COTTON MATHER (I think)
There is no virtue which when carried to excess does not become a vice.

AL WADMAN
When you have children you give hostages to fate.

LOWELL GREENE (about bowling or skating)
Your muscles never forget.

MRS. ELLIOT MONTROLL (when asked by the press what it's like to be married to a genius)
I wouldn't know. Ask my husband

C.B. BROWN
Forget that stuff about saving pennies. Just grab onto a thousand dollars every time you get the chance.

W.C. FIELDS
You can't cheat an honest man.

FANNIE RAFF (speaking of vocations)
There's always room at the top.

RALPH DROSD (about home repairs)
No one will ever again look at your work as carefully as you do when you're finishing it.

HARRY S. TRUMAN
Behind every successful man there's a supportive wife and an incredulous mother-in-law.

AL WADMAN
One sweater is worth $1000 in insulation.

FANNIE RAFF
When I was a girl Fannie was a name, and not something you sat on.

# CHEATING IN COLLEGE

There are two stories I like to tell about cheating on exams in college. The first story has to do with Professor Gus Bischoff, who taught one of our mechanical engineering courses, who was a real fine gent and a good teacher. The other story has to do with a civil engineering class which was not very inspirational. I think it's fair to say that these are the only two instances in which I was involved in or obser ved anything close to cheating.

Bischoff always used to trust the students on exams. He would hand out an exam paper and walk out of the room. Then he would come back towards the end of the hour and pick up the papers. That was always his practice. On this one exam, there was a simple question which had to do with angles and cutting edges. When he handed back the papers, he was really upset. He couldn't resist complaining and lamenting. What he thought was that all these years he had been walking out of the room and the students would cheat on him wholesale. The reason was, that in the course of doing the problem, one got the angle $13°$, which was supposed to be subtracted from 90. As he put it, "Everybody in the class, almost, got the same wrong answer. Everybody subtracted 13 from 90 and got 77. You must be doing the exams cooperatively.

It was breaking his heart, and he was going to have to revise his whole method of teaching. As he went on complaining about this, somebody shouted out from the back of the room: "But Professor Bischoff, 13 from 90 is 77."

He paused for a moment and a big smile spread over his face. I have never seen anybody so relieved.

The other story is more serious, and could have been a disaster for me personally. Among the last exams I took in college was my Civil Engineering final. The teacher was uninspiring and slow talking. He wore thick glasses and had a hearing aid, and must have been in his late seventies. We didn't think very much of him, so there was very little student respect. Besides that, we sat at drafting tables, two to a table. I shared my table with someone named Silverstein, who was, as I recollect, a pretty good student, probably around "B". At one point during the exam he was apparently hung up on some problem, and asked me how to do it. That put me in a rather embarrassing situation because I certainly wasn't going to explain to him, during the exam, how to do the problem; with the teacher sitting up front. I therefore moved my solution to the problem over to the center of the table between us. He took the hint and after a few moments, gathered it in as though it was one of his papers.

I thought he would use it to see how to do the problem. Instead he copied it. I had made some kind of a silly numerical mistake; he made the same mistake. Now the teacher may have been a little blind and deaf, but he wasn't stupid. He knew that the two of us shared a drafting table, and we made the same mistake on the exam.

That was one of my last finals. I took my last exam on Friday, got married on Sunday, and went on my honeymoon. I had a job with General Electric all set up. When I came back from my honeymoon and went to look at my grades, I found that for that particular course, posted on the board next to my name, instead of a grade was posted, "See me."

I went in to see the professor, and fortunately Silverstein had already been in because he had the same thing next to his name. Silverstein had confessed that it was he who was cheating off me. Silverstein was a lower senior and had another 6 months to go. He was required to take the course over the next semester. What would have happened if he hadn't confessed, I don't know. I suspect my career might have been ruined because I might not have gotten my degree, might not have gotten my job with General Electric, and would have had to stay in college another semester. It was a close call.

# MY RUN-IN WITH THE IRS

Some time in the late seventies I got a letter from Internal Revenue to set up an appointment to explain my last year's charitable deductions. After some phone calls I arrived with cancelled checks for all my charities. I was met by a pretty young mulatto girl who took the stack of checks, sat down opposite me at a table and started from the top. There was about $4000 of checks.

The first check was for $2 to WABA. She asked, "What is WABA?" "The Washington Area Bicyclists Association." "Is that a recognized charity?" "I think so — I'm not sure." "I'll look it up," she said as she rose and left the room. After about 20 impatient minutes she came back. "Well, is it?" I asked.

"Someone has the book out and I can't tell, but it's only two dollars." Then she thought the best thing to do was to add up all the checks. It came within a few hundred dollars of what I had claimed. "That's pretty close," she said. "We don't expect it to be exact."

That was it! No adjustments. I got a letter saying my return was okay.

# LETTER OF CONDOLENCE

This is a letter I sent to Selma Sagman when her father, my mother's brother, died about 1970. He must have been close to 80 years old, and died in an auto accident. His daughter in law was driving.

Dear Selma,

I want to offer my condolences to you and Milton and Willy and to tell you that I feel pretty sad too. Your dad was a very special person to me, although Lord knows, I didn't see him very often, and of course I must have had a very different picture than you, seeing him from so much greater distance.

I always considered my mother's genes a marvelous heritage. I think Uncle Harry and Aunt Tess had an extraordinary capacity to feel emotion, a sort of deep "simpatico." In fact I remember as a kid I could always make Uncle Harry cry when I recited "Mother of Mine." As I got a little older I think it embarrassed me a little. I know your Dad had that too, but I've always thought of Uncle Herman as the Boulevardier of the family, the gay blade, and the charmer. How my mother loved to show him off. More than me even!

She told me about the last time he came to visit her on Jesup Avenue; how she introduced him to the ladies sitting around outside, and how he gave each one that little personal charm treatment that only your father could. She was so proud to have him as a brother that she lit up as she told me about it. I could visualize Uncle Herman shaking each old lady's hand and extending himself to say the flattering thing and make a little gay remark (maybe even off color), and enjoying every minute of it because he knew it delighted his sister Fannie, and it came so naturally to him. I can visualize the old ladies talking about

Fannie Raff's brother after he left, or at least I can visualize my mother visualizing it, which is more to the point.

Selma - I'm afraid we've come to the end of an era. That generation of Sagmans is almost gone. Even my mother is almost gone. She has her good moments, but the world overwhelms her so easily. It's sad, but I guess this is the time for sadness.

How about us? When you feel a little more removed, write me a little newsy letter about Berl & your family, & I'll do the same. I'm not in the mood for a newsy letter now, & I'm sure you're not in the mood to read one. Maybe one day we'll even see each other again. Everyone has to come to The Lincoln Memorial at some time.

Love & Sad Nostalgia,

Sammie

# RIGGS & METZEROTT ROADS IN HYATTSVILLE

In 1950 Lillian and I bought a house out in the country at Riggs and Metzerott Roads in Hyattsville. The house stood all alone at a "T" intersection so that Metzerott Road would run through the living room if it were extended. Someplace I found out in 1953 that the gas company was running a line through the intersection, and I thought it would be cheaper than the bottle gas we were using. I called and asked them to hook me up when they came through.

There weren't any street signs in my immediate vicinity, but that was the mailing address we used. Going east on Metzerott road from my house it branched after about 1/4 mile. The south branch was Old Colesville Road, and going south on Riggs Road it took a fairly sharp curve. Somewhere to the north Riggs Road changed names to Powder Mill Road.

The gas company informed me that the intersection of Riggs and Metzerott Roads was half a mile to the southwest of my house. I lived on Old Colesville and Powder Mill Roads — and they were right according to the official map. What's more, Hyattsville ended south of us and we were in Berwyn. After that it was harder for me to find my way home from work.

For the record, The Citizens Association later changed the name of that part of Powder Mill Road to Riggs Road and the name of Old Colesville Road to Adelphi Road.

# THE DIRTY WORD

When I was a little boy, and you'll have to guess how little from the context of the story because that's the only way I can guess; we frequently spent part of each summer at a place called Kober's Farm. It was really a sort of second rate guest hotel where women brought their children and the husbands came up on weekends.

It was customary at Kober's Farm that the children ate first. I can't remember whether we had a separate dining room or all ate in the same dining room, children first before they cleared it off while we went out to play. At any rate, the scene that I'm about to describe took place with a lot of kids of various ages seated at a long table with food being stuffed into them. At one point in this proceeding some kid shouted a very dirty word, namely, "fuck." There was a moment of shocked silence, during which I upstaged everyone by saying, "And I know what it means."

At this point the silence was so deep that it seemed it would never end. But my mother, who was standing next to me came in after a moment with the statement, "All right, smarty-pants, what, does it mean?"

Everybody was listening carefully, and I had to admit that I really didn't know what it meant, although I had heard it before and I knew it was a very, very dirty word.

# MY MOTHER

Fannie Raff was born in Europe, someplace near Minsk, although my father at one time or another accused her of deceiving him into believing that she was born in The United States. Certainly she could deceive anyone because she had not the slightest trace of an accent. In fact, my mother, as a young woman, was a secretary in the days when woman secretaries were pretty rare. She was an excellent typist, and certainly as far as I was concerned, the world's greatest authority on spelling and punctuation.

She was older than my father by several years. I never knew how many. It was a disgrace in those days for a woman to be older than her husband, and it was kept secret from us children. So secret, in fact, that there was even some uncertainty about my mother's birthday. I remember when she died my Uncle Alex said, "Oh, everybody knew Fannie was older than Nat." She always avoided telling her age, or lied about it, and I recall that long after my father was dead, when Elaine and Lenny were taking care of her in Middletown, Lenny commented that one of the doctors, an associate of his, said that her tissues looked much older than her age.

After my father died, my mother went to work at the Bronx County courthouse in some sort of a civil service job that was gotten for her through political influence by an old school chum named Lazarous Joseph. My mother contacted him at some time in the thirties when things were pretty bad for the Raffs economically, as they were for many people at that time. He was the Comptroller of the city, and doing very well. I'll tell you more about him later. In any case, she maintained a friendship with him, and after my father died, he got her this Job at City Hall in The Bronx. When I needed a passport for my first trip to Europe, I had to have a birth certificate in order to get it. I lived in Washington at the time and I called my mother and told her, "You're right there in the courthouse, where they keep the records, just send me a copy of my birth certificate."

She was horrified. No, she could never do that because on my birth certificate it would have her age, and she lied about her age when she got her job, and they would all find out and she would be fired. What's more, she forbade me from requesting one through normal channels because the request would come up into that office where she worked and they would see her age on the birth certificate and she would lose her job. So what I had to do was get an affidavit of birth which she signed for me under the pretext that they couldn't find my birth certificate in the courthouse. Afterwards I figured out that she wasn't worried about losing her job, but she was afraid of my finding out about her age. It was all connected to her having lied about it through her whole life. In fact, my birth certificate does not have her age on it, but she thought it did.

She kept the job at City Hall for a long time, commuting to work on the subway. Then one day they had a big black-out in New York. The subway stopped, and they had to take everybody out in the dark with lanterns and walk them along the tracks. That experience was so harrowing to her at her age, which was probably her late seventies, that she never went to work or went into the subway again.

As she grew older, my mother was baffled by the simplest things. I recall that she had a hearing aid that sometimes she could not get into her ear in the proper position. When she came to stay with us sometimes on Aragon Lane she would sleep in what I called the ag-room. That was short for aggravation. I'll tell you about that later. But the switch for the light in that room was outside the door, right next to it, but outside. I would hate to tell you how many times she could not find that switch and had to come for help to turn out the light. At her end she was in a nursing home in New Jersey where Elaine was the principal person who took care of her and watched over her and knew about her. I can recall receiving a phone call from Elaine with great enthusiasm. She thought Mom was getting better because this time when she visited, Mom recognized her.

Through most of her life, or the part that I remember, she was a woman who had lots and lots of friends and loved to play bridge and Mah-Jongg. She was a marvelous cook, although my father loved to tell the story about when they were first married and he found her shelling string beans for dinner. Every once in a while we would have hot dogs for dinner, and I would always say they were great. I liked them, and my mother would always say, "Great! You do? Then we'll have them twice a week." Then, three weeks later we would have them again.

I remember Irving Cohen. He had a truck from which he would sell fruits and vegetables through the neighborhood. In fact I worked for him for one or two summers. I got $3 per week. I would help carry the packages and weigh things, and I even got to the point where I could take cash. I think I must have been in public school, or maybe just starting in high school at the time. At any rate, I always thought that Irving had a real crush on my mother. That, and the fact that we had a large family and she was a good cook, and he liked to go home early; often led to a scene where my mother would show up around 2 in the afternoon when Irving was itching to go home, and he would start unloading on her all the vegetables that he had left over and couldn't keep for tomorrow. He would sell her huge quantities of things for 10c or 25c and we would have vegetable dinners. I liked them. My mother would make 5 or 6 different kinds of vegetables. She always cooked them well, and they were always very good. She was very proud about preparing spinach. I heard her say many times that when she prepares spinach she cleans each leaf separately. And indeed she did. She took each leaf of spinach under the sink and got the sand out of all the cracks.

There was no doubt in my mind too, that Morris Frank had a crush on my mother. I think that one was reciprocated. Morris had 3 boys, the youngest of which was about a year older than me, and for a long time was my bosom buddy. His name was Leon. They lived for a while on the same floor as us in an apartment house on 179th Street. It was right across the street from the school. Leon was not only a year older than me, but considerably bigger. I was a shrimp, until about my 15th birthday when I started catching up in size with all the boys my age. Morris, the father, was a tall and very good looking man with a moustache I can't recall any specific instances which made me think there was something between him and my mother, but I often thought so. His wife, whose first name I don't remember, was a rather good cook, and I ate there often, being a close friend of Leon. I remember on one occasion Mrs. Frank made coleslaw and I thought it was really magnificent. I told my mother enthusiastically about this coleslaw. Her reaction was interesting. She said, "Oh? I'll get the recipe from Mrs. Frank." And for the rest of her life, she often made the same coleslaw that Mrs. Frank had made.

One characteristic of my mother's cooking was that there was always a profusion of vegetables, and more often than not one of them would remain on the stove to be remembered only after dinner was finished. Then she would upbraid herself briefly for forgetting and ask why we didn't remind her. Sometimes we did by asking when she finished putting food on the table, "Did you forget a vegetable?" Usually there was one left on the stove.

The left over vegetables were rarely wasted however. I developed a great fondness for using them in my scrambled eggs at breakfast. In fact I loved all kinds of leftovers in my morning scrambled eggs, particularly spaghetti.

During most of the period I can remember, my father spent a lot of his time "on the road." That usually meant out selling combs someplace within automobile travel distance, like Chicago or Cleveland; places which added up to trips of perhaps a week's duration. I remember traveling to New Haven with him once on a one day trip. There was a factory there which was making hard rubber combs for him. I guess they were his molds. There's a big story about molds in the thirties and hard rubber combs, and I'll tell you about that later.

I recall that I was staying with Leon Frank when Elaine was born. It was Mrs. Frank that told me that I had a new sister. This came to me as a total surprise. I know I was 9 years old, and it's hard for me to believe that I could have been that unobservant as not to notice that my mother was pregnant, but those are the facts as I recall them.

An extraordinary fact about my mother Is that Elaine was born in 1929; my father was born in 1885; therefore my father was 44 years old when Elaine was born, and my mother was older than him by some, uncertain number of years. Aside from the biological factors, they could not have been overjoyed at the prospect of having a fourth child when times were getting tough. We lived in a two bedroom apartment, a very nice apartment, but still, all three of us children shared a bedroom. And yet there is not the slightest doubt in the mind of anyone in the family that Elaine turned out to be the jewel of their later life. She's the one who took care of them and knew where they were all the time and worried about their welfare and their shopping. And besides, she's the one that always kept the family together and still does.

Elaine was a brat and we older kids always complained about her to my mother. For example it was usual for her to go out of her way to 'accidentally' step on Eli's white shoes when he came to court Sylvia. One day I recall saying to Mom, "You're spoiling that child; spoiling her rotten."

My mother replied, "That's how I raise my children. I spoiled you too. Now go away and let me take care of my business."

It was many, many years after that that I wandered into my parents' bedroom one night and found them unmistakably engaged in sexual acts. I was old enough to be quite certain of what was happening, yet young enough to be shocked. Maybe surprised is a better word than shocked.

# LAZAROUS JOSEPH

Lazarous Joseph had been a high school friend of my mother. I really don't know how close they were, but he got into politics and became Comptroller of the city of New York. I think my mother called him up to congratulate him on his election, and afterwards there was some friendship between him and our family. I recall that there were several occasions when he came over to the house in the afternoon to play bridge with my mother, my brother Eddie and me.

I don't recall much about his bridge playing capability, but I do recall a discussion we once had about money. This must have been about 1936, when things were really tough for everybody, although we lived in a rather nice house: 1545 Jesup Avenue in The Bronx. I recall he was saying that he was in a financial bind and couldn't seem to get his expenses down to his income. Now, among his expenses, I recall, was a chauffeur, and 50c cigars of which he smoked about 3 or 4 a day. Now a rapid computation indicates that four 50c cigars a day is $14 a week, in a period of time when there were a lot of people supporting families on less than that.

The extraordinary thing about the discussion was that he made his case very well. As far as cigars were concerned, that was a brand of cigars that he really liked and had been smoking for many years. He would sooner give up smoking than smoke anything else. His chauffeur was really essential to his way of life because, he pointed out, he had a lot of business appointments in town and a lot of places to go, and if he had to rely on public transportation and it rained, he couldn't get a taxicab. Therefore he would have to schedule his appointments very much farther apart to allow time to park his car, and wait in parking lots for it to come out. It would slow down his whole ability to do business. A chauffeur was, to him, an essential item.

That was the first time I realized how easy it is to get adjusted to a standard of living, and how hard it is to cut down on your expenses no matter how lavish they may seem to someone from a different skein of life. I remembered that recently in connection with the Arab oil revenue and the recent drop in oil prices.

# UNCLE LOUIE

Uncle Louie was the first husband of my Aunt Jeanette, my father's younger sister. Uncle Louie was in the silk business, and did very well by our family's standards, although I have no idea how wealthy he really was. He was some significant years older than Aunt Jeanette, and she afterwards said that she never really loved the man, but the marriage was arranged by the families. She had two children by him, Marian and Selma. I think at one time they all went to law school together, Jeanette and the two children. There was some publicity about the mother and daughter team.

Uncle Louie had a fairly thick foreign accent, like many Jewish immigrants. Their English progresses to a certain point and then doesn't improve no matter how long they stay here. Uncle Louie and my father loved to play rummy. They would sit down at every opportunity and play rummy for a nickel a game, or a nickel for knock rummy and ten cents for rummy-out. They could play for hours and hours and insult each other with the greatest good humor. The classic remark which I remember coming mostly from Uncle Louie as he put down a card was, "I'm gonna give you an aggravation party."

At any rate, the extraordinary thing about Uncle Louie was that when my father's sister Jeanette divorced him, he came to live with us. In fact he shared my bedroom for a while. At the time the strangeness of this didn't quite reach me. It was by no means a friendly divorce. Although Jeanette always said she bore him no ill will and she wished him all the best, that was not his viewpoint about it at all. He often would spend hours complaining and threatening to give her an aggravation party. How my father quite took this I don't know, but he seemed to accept it with equanimity. I never really heard him agree with Louie against his own sister. He certainly remained friendly with his sister. I think they just let Louie complain without agreeing or disagreeing. Louie threatened to have Jeanette disbarred. At that time she was already a lawyer. This had something to do with the fact that it was a Mexican divorce, which was not quite legal somehow. She had shortly thereafter remarried. She married Tom Johnson, and I must say a few things about him later.

Uncle Louie always took the full blame for the divorce. I heard him say a thousand times in almost the same words, "It's all my fault," and then qualify it with the brief explanation, "I was too good to that woman." Needless to say, Uncle Louie got over it after a while, and lived to a ripe old age with a new wife.

# ELI'S 70th BIRTHDAY PARTY — NOVEMBER 1983

Sylvia asked me to raise a toast. After a little thought I said, "Here's to a man who has been miserably unhappy in some of the best jobs in the country and who has slept in better company than anyone I can think of."

My cousin Helen (Klebenoff) daughter of my mother's sister Tess was there and she told me three stories she remembers about my brother Eddie. One was that when he was at DeWitt Clinton High School and doing badly, my mother suggested to the principal that it was because there were no girls there for him to show off for. Clinton was an all boy's school. He was transferred to Evander Childs which was mixed, and he did much better. I'm not sure that's true.

The second story is about how my folks made a long hard trip to visit him at a summer camp, walked a mile to the other side of the campus to find him at basketball and got as a greeting a quick, "Hi - nice to see you - I gotta go down to the lake now. Bye!"

The third story is about his not staying in bed when he had diphtheria.

Helen is delightful, but a little strange. When her children (Todd and Fran) went to school she didn't want them vaccinated because, as she put it to my mother, "Their blood is pure, Fanny — it shouldn't be polluted with chemicals."

At some time in the distant past Helen taught me a song which I taught to some of my kids:

Once I went in swimming where there were no women
In the deep blue sea
Seeing no one there I hung my underwear
Upon a willow tree
I dove into the water just like Pharaoh's daughter

Dove into the Nile
But someone saw me there and stole my underwear
And left me in a smile.

# MY SISTERS-IN-LAW

I had two sisters-in-law. One was an expert on all subjects. The other was the world's foremost authority.

# UNCLE SIDNEY

Uncle Sidney was my father's youngest brother, the youngest of five boys and two girls. When I remember him he had a round pot belly, smoked cigars and drove a cab. He was married to a woman named Sophie who was greatly admired by the family because she arranged his socks neatly in the drawer. They had no children. He spent some time in a mental institution, during which time Sophie remarried. Uncle Alex said at one time that they would release him but there was no one to take care of him. He died about 1970.

I like to remember him for a joke I heard him tell several times. "Do you know why I keep the band on my cigar?" ——

"Because I appreciate music."

# BIKINI

Before Bikini was a bathing suit, it was a coral atoll in the western Pacific where we tested our 4th and 5th atomic bombs against ships. The first bomb we fired at Alamogordo, New Mexico on a tower, to see if the concept really worked. The second and third bombs were dropped on Hiroshima and Nagasaki to encourage the Japanese to end the war. The fourth and fifth bombs were tested at Bikini atoll right after the war ended.

I was one of the scientists, engineers and 40,000 other people involved in the tests. I still have my Identification card with my picture on it. God, how young I was! It was issued on the 20th of March 1946 to expire on the 1st of September of the same year.

It was called Project Crossroads and the Task Force was called the Atomic Bomb Task Force I (Joint). The card is signed by Vice Admiral Blandy who was the commander of Joint Task Force I. I also still have one of the radiation dosimeters which they issued, although I think this was not the one issued to me because it has another name on it. It's just like the one I carried. It looks a little bit like a short stubby fountain pen, and you carried it around in your pocket. They charged it every week, and then you brought it in at the end of the week and you were told how much radiation you had been exposed to. You could look at it and see, so that you didn't have to actually bring it back to find out how much radiation you had been exposed to.

We also had some badges which they would develop to check our exposure. They were photographic, but they constituted another check on the dosage that you had been exposed to. Of course, that was the ambient dosage. If, perchance some radioactive material got into your body somehow, they really had no good way of checking that out. In those days we weren't very sophisticated about radiation. We knew it was bad, and we knew it should be checked. I have no idea what sorts of levels were considered tolerable. I strongly suspect, however, that what was considered tolerable in those days is pretty far from what's acceptable today.

When the war ended, the Navy had a lot of ships, ours and captured ships, which it had no use for. The Navy also had a great need to learn more about the affects of atomic weapons. They therefore arranged the Bikini test, which consisted of two atomic explosions, one in the air at a height of a few thousand feet, and the other 100 ft under the water. These bombs were tested against an array of about 50 ships which were anchored in the lagoon of the Bikini atoll.

An atoll is a ring of coral islands which is very common because of the method of formation of coral. The formation starts with a mountain peak, like a volcanic peak, which is at the surface or close to it in a tropical area. By close, I mean less than 200 feet from the surface. Under these circumstances, coral will start to form. It doesn't form much deeper than that because the sunlight does not penetrate farther. Coral either requires sunlight or feeds upon organisms that require sunlight. It also requires wave action to bring oxygenated water to the little coral organisms. When these conditions are right, the coral starts to multiply and deposit its shells. Presently other coral starts to form on top of the shells of the dead coral, and you have coral rock formations which are porous and can be very, very large. Because wave action is required, the coral will form almost to the surface and then more coral will grow on the seaward side. But the coral on the inside of the formation tends to die because, although there is water there, the water is not moving and agitating and is not bringing oxygen to the coral.

The result of this process is that if you start with a single peak which is close to the surface, the coral rock tends to form a big cap on top of that peak and actually overhangs the peak if the peak is steep. After a while the overhanging pieces get very massive because more and more coral is forming on the outside. They will then break off and roll down the slope and then the process starts over again, and another huge piece of coral will break off and roll down the slope. Presently, in that way, the peak becomes wider and the coral keeps moving out. After many centuries you end up with a ring of coral sitting on top of broken pieces. In the center, where the peak was originally, the coral tends to dissolve and wash away. Fresh coral can't grow there because the wave action is blocked by the ring on the outside. This is the general process by which a coral atoll is formed. The water at the center is usually fairly shallow. In the Bikini Atoll, the center part, the lagoon, was about 200' deep. The ring of Islands around it was not continuous, but it was about 20 miles in diameter with gaps between islands. The largest island was called Bikini, and it was probably about 2 or 3 miles long and about 1/2 mile wide at the widest place. A lot of the other islands in the atoll had names. One of them that I remember was Aerokiji.

The natives, who were gone when we arrived (they had been moved elsewhere) used to live only on Bikini. Aerokiji was an Island they went to, sort of on vacation. It was a somewhat smaller island than Bikini, and just about on the opposite side of the lagoon. I guess they went there when the food supply began to diminish a little bit on Bikini. The food supply being birds that they caught somehow, coconuts, fish that lived in the lagoon and on the seaward side of the island too, and to a very large extent, shellfish.

I recall my trip to Aerokiji Island; we went in a little motor launch. They couldn't bring the launch into the beach because it was too rough. So I swam ashore, and then we brought a rubber boat in. The beach was covered with giant clam shells and I thought it would be nice to bring one back as a souvenir. But they were incredibly heavy, and the one I finally did bring back was a good size for an ashtray. I tried to bring back one that was about the size of a large dinner plate, but it weighed probably about 60 lbs. At first I tried to bring back an even larger one, but I couldn't even drag that one along the beach. I still have the ashtray. It's in my office; an incredibly solid piece of stone.

One of the most memorable things about the trip to Aerokiji Island was that swimming in to the beach, the water was so clear that I kept thinking that I could stand up. I could clearly see some beautiful open flowerlike things on the bottom. Fortunately, the water was about three times as deep as I thought it was. I say fortunately, because those beautiful flowerlike things were giant clams lying open and if I had been able to reach the bottom, that would have been the end of me. One of them would have closed on my foot and either cut it clean off, or trapped me below the surface where I would soon drown.

My outstanding recollection of the tests themselves was that none of the scientific equipment or instruments which we brought with us worked. Further, despite great efforts, everything was terribly disorganized. I was in the underwater test group. We deployed, around the ships, some gauges with which to measure the shock pressures under the water. We did this both for the air blast and for the underwater blast. The gauges were very simple devices. They were called ball-crusher gauges and they consisted of two cylinders which screwed together with a ball and a piston. The pressure acted on the piston and compressed the ball. After the test was over, you recovered the device, took the ball out and measured how much it had been dented by the piston. This was a measure of the pressure. The device had been tested many, many times with ordinary explosions, and was properly calibrated. The only real problem was getting the devices back after the test.

We deployed the ball crusher gauges in strings about 10 ft apart, cabled together. What were actually cabled together were about 20 square steel plates about 6 inches square and half an inch thick, each of which had four gauges screwed into it near the corners. We had an anchor at the bottom and floats at the top of the string in order to get them back at the end of the test. The floats at the top consisted of two items. One was an empty oil drum, and in case that was crushed or destroyed, we also had a rubber life raft. In case that was also crushed or destroyed, we had all these vertical strings chained together along the bottom of the lagoon. This was so that if we recovered one string, we could pull on this chain along the bottom and recover the others.

The first test, the air test, crushed all the oil drums and shattered the life rafts, but the chain which held all the strings together on the bottom worked, and as soon as we had a diver go down and find one of them, we could pull then all up. However, the underwater pressure was so low that we had nothing to measure. That is, we couldn't find any dents in the balls.

On the second test, the underwater test, we had lots of dents in the balls. The oil drums and the life rafts were gone as before, but after we sent a diver down to find one and started pulling on the chain to get the other strings, we soon discovered that the blast had stirred up the coral sand on the bottom of the lagoon, and this had settled back over the chain and it was about as hard as cement. We broke the chain again and again and had to send divers down to get each string. Some strings we never recovered. But we did get some results, although with great difficulty.

The air blast group was not nearly as lucky. Their principal instrumentation was what was called pots. These were essentially steel plates with holes of different sizes. You put a sheet of aluminum foil over the plate and the air pressure would punch out the aluminum foil. It took a lower pressure to punch out the big holes and a higher pressure to punch out the small holes. Therefore by knowing which holes were punched out, you would know what the pressure was at any particular point. The problem with that was that the salt spray, which was everywhere, just eroded those aluminum sheets to the point that there was nothing left for the air pressure to punch out. They also had a marvelous device which was supposed to measure the pressure as a function of time. It was a very freely moving piston which the pressure would start moving. The piston had a little stylus on it which was supposed to make a line on a piece of paper wrapped around a rotating drum. I recall they set these all out before the test (about 2 weeks before) and then they went around checking them to see if they were working. They were all frozen up due to corrosion. So they cleaned them and oiled them, one at a time, and got them working again. Then they'd go on to the next one. Clean that, oil it, get it working. To the next one, and so on. They continued with the process right up until the test, and I don't think they ever found one of them that was working when they got to it. It really didn't much matter though, because the rotating drum had to be started by a radio signal, and that was never given. Besides, if it had been given, it could not have been received because the black boxes that were supposed to receive the radio signal (they contained rather delicate electronics and were ventilated) were welded on the ship's bulkheads close to the deck, and if anybody had gotten up early enough in the morning, they would have found out that the crew of every ship washed them down with salt water every morning. They never had a chance. So, that particular experiment failed for three reasons, any one of which was overwhelming.

The funniest thing, however, was what we called the pyramidal orientometers. These were devices shaped like a pyramid, made out of sheet metal, with a hole in the top. Inside, at the base, was a pine board. Their objective was to determine where the bomb went off with respect to each of the ships in the air blast case. (The ships were swinging at their moorings.) The Idea of the pyramidal orientometer was that the radiation from the bomb would go through the little hole in the top of the pyramid and char a spot on the pine board at the base. Then, from where that spot was on the base, one could determine the direction of the explosion relative to the ship. The principal was great, and I helped them solve certain geometry problems relative to the fact that the orientometers were sitting at funny angles.

I helped them before the air blast, but it was all of no avail because after the air blast there were no char marks on the pine boards. The paint on the ships was charred. You could see shadows of ladders, and there were generally char marks all over the target ships, but there were none on the pine bases of the pyramidal orientometers.

What's more, the char marks on the ships were not consistent at all in indicating which direction the blast came from. I recall seeing a ladder on the side of the ship which cast a shadow in char against the paint on the side of the ship, and it was clear that the shadow was in an upward direction, as though the bomb had gone off under the surface of the water.

The conclusion I reached, and I'm pretty firm about this, is that the char was really not due to the radiation at all, but was due to the shock wave; that is, the shock wave associated with the blast compresses the air adiabatically, and that compression raises the air temperature to the point that it chars the paint. I checked with several people afterwards, and in fact with Dr. Hartmann, who headed the air blast group, and is a close friend and employee of mine. No one I contacted ever heard that theory or understood why the orientometers didn't work.

The bombs they tested at Bikini were 20 Kiloton size, the same size they used at Hiroshima and Nagasaki. Later they tested a 60 megaton bomb in The Pacific; 3000 times as large. The bombs I saw were quite impressive. A lot of ships were sunk. However, sinking an unmanned ship is quite a different thing from sinking a ship with a crew on it. Most of the ships sunk went down hours or days later, so that if they had had power up and could pump or put out fire, they might not have sunk.

Two particular cases in point were the carrier Saratoga and the Japanese battleship Nagato. The Saratoga had a load of munitions aboard and the bomb started a fire which got to the munitions after about 12 hours. When they blew, they peeled back the rear half of the deck like a can opener and the ship sank in minutes.

The Nagato was an 18 inch battleship built by the Japanese during the period of the arms limitation treaties, and it was supposed to be 35,000 tons gross weight. Our battleship Nevada, which was at the center of the array of target ships, was 35,000 tons, and it looked like a rowboat alongside the Nagato. The armor plate on the Nagato's deck house was 18 inches thick, and when you looked through slits in the plate it was like looking through a tunnel. It had torpedo blisters on its sides (to prevent torpedoes from reaching the main hull.) They were wide enough for four people to walk abreast. In fact I met my old Physics Professor George Gamow while strolling on one of those blisters. The underwater blast sank the Nagato, but only a week after the blast. Surely if a crew had been aboard, they could have saved her. It's strange how fast a ship deteriorates without a crew. No one was willing to go into the Nagato below deck spaces even before the bombs. The ladders were slimy, and the ship was alleged to be full of rats.

The Nagato never really got into the war because it was at the dock being repaired almost continuously. We would bomb it from time to time to keep it there. The final blow was a 500 lb bomb that one of our aviators skipped into an aircraft hangar on the deck. That sprung the ship so badly that the Japanese gave up on repairing it.

It is hard for me to tell how close the individual ships were to the bomb because they were swinging at their moorings. The underwater bomb was moored in the lagoon, but the air blast bomb was dropped by a B-29. It missed the center of the array by about half a mile despite the fact that the weather was clear and magnificent, and the Nevada, at the

center of the array, was painted red.

It was a great adventure though. I got to spend three months on shipboard. I was on the USS Wharton almost all that time. That had been a luxury liner called The Southern Cross which was converted during the war to a troop carrier. It was an Incredibly Impressive sized ship, 20,000 tons. When I first boarded it in San Francisco, they were loading beer. Forty thousand cases of beer. Now that's just a number until you see the flat cars pull up alongside of the ship. People load cases of beer into a cargo net.

The cargo net goes down into the hold and gets unloaded while they bring up another cargo net. This process went on all day and night for 3 days. I thought we were carrying beer for the whole task force. Apparently not. Other ships were carrying beer also. They set up an Officers Club and an Enlisted Mans Club on Bikini Island, and all that beer was consumed before we got back.

A lot of other alcoholic beverages were consumed too. In fact a shipmate of mine was a navy gunner named Orr. When we left Hawaii, which was our first stop after San Francisco, Orr brought aboard enormous quantities of hard liquor, which he asked everybody to help him store. There was not supposed to be any hard liquor on shipboard, or indeed, any alcoholic beverages of any kind. I recall I had 3 fifths of bourbon, in my locker for him. He was drunk from the time we left Hawaii until the time I left The Wharton, about 2 1/2 months later. The last I heard of him was, after we got back. There was an announcement on the radio that everybody that had been on the atomic bomb tests should come in for radiation checks because someone had died. At first I was really frightened by this, but in a later repeat of the announcement they gave the name of the person who had died. It was gunner's mate Orr. I didn't even bother to go in for a check.

I watched the air blast from 10 miles away through a device called an Icaroscope, which was intended to protect my eyes. Honestly, I don't know what I saw at the instant that the bomb went off because immediately afterwards we compared notes among all the observers on the ship and everybody saw something different. Later, when I saw movies of the blast, I saw something different again. I knew the 10 mile distance was adequate because a little closer to the bomb than me there was a command ship that was reputed to have aboard 57 Admirals and Generals.

I watched the underwater blast with my naked eye from 5 miles away. I do know what I saw. I saw this cylinder of what looked like spray rise up out of the lagoon, and I saw a ship rise up with it. I 'm not sure what ship that was, but that cylinder of spray went up for a long time. It seemed like 10 seconds or more that it kept rising. After that it peaked out and started back down again, indicating that it was not spray at all, but more like solid water. After that I could watch the progress of the shock wave through the water as it came toward us, by the line of flying fish which jumped. This line of fish came closer and closer to us until they reached the ship itself. At that point there was a ping in the ship's plating. It was, apparently, the shock wave that was causing the fish to jump out of the water.

All through our trip through The Pacific I remember seeing the flying fish jumping and sort of sailing out of the way of the bow wave. Another thing I remember seeing in the water as we traveled through The Pacific was luminescence at night. Apparently the motion of the ship through the water agitated it and caused certain organisms, maybe bacteria, maybe larger things, to glow so that when you looked into the water from the side of the ship there seemed to be a distinct glow at night. The water seemed to be incredibly blue.

After the first few days on shipboard we got tired of watching the luminescence and stars at night and the flying fish in the daytime. We started a bridge game, and that was the thing that soured me on bridge. I think we must have played bridge an average of 8 hours a day, seven days a week for 2 months. It was simply too much.

I was working toward my Ph.D. at the time, or thinking about it, and I knew I had to take language exams in French and German. I had, therefore, brought along a German reader. I worked on the reader at odd times for the first few weeks, and then it disappeared. I never knew what became of it, and there was no way I could get another in that isolated environment.

They showed movies almost every night. The only one I remember was Gilda with Rita Hayworth and Glen Ford. That was a very sexy movie. I saw it about 3 times on the trip, starting when I had been at sea for about a month and was very susceptible to sexy suggestions. To this day I consider that the sexiest movie I have ever seen, but I have to recognize that having been at sea for that length of time, I was very susceptible.

Some of the people I remember spending time with on the trip were Ed Trounson, who I worked for; Ralph Drosd, whose wife bought a house in Avenel, right near our house on Riggs Road while he was at sea with me. It was a new wife, and we would tease him about Avenel being a black area; A.B. Allen, who helped me with my German when I had the book and later went to work with The State Dept.; and Spike Coles who had been my Chemistry teacher at CCNY, and afterwards wrote a book about shock waves and became President of Bowdoin College and later President of The Research Corporation, which is a University affiliated corporation in New York City which licenses patents developed at universities.

I remember that at some stage in the trip we got mail from the states indicating that Charlotte Staton, who was later to become Ed Trounson's 1st wife, and who he was very much in love with at the time, had been hospitalized. Ed wanted to send an urgent message inquiring about the details of the hospitalization, and how she was doing, etc. He explained the situation to the Message Officer on the shipboard, and it was approved for urgency. Then he wrote his message, and it went to another officer, who decided it was too long and told him to shorten it up. It ended up saying something like, "How are you?" Whereupon, somehow, somebody sent it back for another urgency check, and it looked like an ordinary message of greetings and was rejected. By this time I think 3 days had passed; Ed was furious, and he gave up the whole idea. It turned out that there was nothing seriously wrong with Charlotte; and, in fact, they were divorced sometime in the late 1950s and at this point she still seems to be in adequate health, despite a mastectomy.

However Ed has died.

# SPIKE COLES

Spike Coles was my high school Chemistry teacher and also the faculty advisor for Briggs House, to which I belonged as an undergraduate at City College. The college had a house plan instead of fraternities, and there were various "houses" sharing the same building. None of us lived on campus, and we would have meetings and parties on different nights. Spike wasn't much older than the students.

He delivered the Chemistry lectures in a big lecture theater, and they were clear, concise and very understandable, and I thought I was doing very well in Chemistry. My mid-term grade was in the high nineties. We also had laboratory once a week, and at these laboratory sessions he would pass out little yellow pieces of paper and we would take a brief exam; usually 10 questions. At these I did very badly because I never read the book. In fact, I never bought the book because the lectures were so good that the few times I went to the library and got the book and looked at it, it was just repeating what was in the lectures, and I didn't see any need for it. I think my average grade on those little yellow sheets of paper was probably about 40%, but I didn't take them seriously.

Near the end of the term I went to see Spike as a formality to ask him what grade I needed on the final to get an A. He told me I needed about 172% because he averaged in these little yellow exam papers. I was horrified and protested that the whole object of the course was to teach the subject; and I knew the subject. I had learned it, so I should get a good grade. I reminded him that I had been in the high nineties on the mid-term, and as I recalled, that was the highest grade in the class. It became apparent to me in the course of the discussion, that he thought I had cheated on the midterm. Surely I couldn't have copied from anybody because there wasn't anybody who got as high a grade.

He didn't actually accuse me of cheating; it was just something in the discussion that led me to think he felt that way. We ended up agreeing that I would sit right up front when I took the final exam, and if I got over 90 on the final exam, he would give me an A in the course. Not only that, but he was so confident that he also offered to buy me a malted milk in Schraft's if I got over 90. The outcome was that I got the A and he bought me dinner and also bought dinner for Lucille, who I was dating at the time. I thought that was a great victory, and Spike and I were friends ever since. He moves around in Navy circles, and every few years I meet him someplace.

# THE AUTOGRAPH BOOK

I have an old autograph book. I don't know whether or not they still have them, but in my day, when you graduated, all your fellow graduates would try to write something very clever in your book and sign it. You would do the same for them, and the teachers would write, usually, very profound statements like, "Sincerely, Charles A. Brueg." I have an autograph book which is a bit of a gem for two reasons.

First of all, there is a page with the following statement from my sister, Sylvia: "You better develop into some kind of a mental genius or your family will have no way of explaining your absentmindedness." What a comfort that page has been to me in my old age. I am terribly absentminded, and every time I tend to blame that on age, I remember that marvelous page that my sister filled out, and I know that I have always been that way. In fact it reminds me that my mother used to have my brown bag lunch ready for me when I went to school, and she always handed it to me as I went out the apartment door. Her claim was that if she handed it to me 3 steps back, I would be distracted, get involved in something else, put it down and forget to pick it up when I left.

The other gem is a page from my younger sister, Elaine. On it is written in my hand:

"Happiness I wish to you, Health, wealth & long life too — your sister, Elaine"

And then there is her own personal writing contribution which consists of an X next to the name Elaine and a vertical series of numbers, 1, backwards 3, a 4, a 5, a backwards 6, an upside down 7, an 8, a back-wards 10 and a forwards 10. I produced this page of the autograph book at a family gathering at one time, and Elaine took it in a very strange way. It took me a little while before I realized what she was saying, which was essentially that all children are not very bright. She was being very defensive, but was greatly relieved when I pointed out to her that it was not my high school autograph book, but my junior high school autograph book; she was only 5 years old then. She had automatically assumed it was my high school autograph book and her mental calculations revealed that she must have been about 8 years old at the time.

# YIDDISH

As a boy in The Bronx, the people around me, particularly at home, tended to sprinkle Yiddish words in with their English, particularly when they were upset or angry. The result is that I was always a little bit confused as a child about which words were Yiddish. I remember being startled by hearing one of my teachers use the word aggravation. I had always thought that was a Jewish word because of the context in which my mother used it. I also remember one time my buddy, Leon Frank played a big joke on me by asking me what the Yiddish word for Luckshion was.

My mother's mother, who was the only grandparent I can recollect, spoke only Yiddish. That put me at a great disadvantage in trying to warm up to her. She lived with my Uncle Harry, my mother's brother, and his wife Rose. I guess she helped Rose take care of the house and the children, although, during the period of her life that I remember, she was really getting peculiar. I was told that when Harry was not at home she would follow Rose around the house as she did her cleaning to make sure that Rose didn't steal anything from her husband. I do know that every once in a while my mother would get a frantic call from Rose, "Please take her Fanny, for just a few days. I promise, I'll take her back on Wednesday, but I've just got to have a little time with her out of the house so I can collect myself together again."

On those occasions we took her for a few days, but that was a problem because she was strictly kosher and we were not. In fact, Harry was the only one in my mother's family who kept a kosher house.

Bubby would come with her little pot, in which she would hard boil eggs, and bring her own spoons and plates, which she kept separate. Even when she stayed with us, I'm afraid I had very little contact with her because of the language difficulty.

I could never manage more than a few words of Yiddish, and nothing very coherent. As a matter of fact, much later in life I used the word momser to a neighbor, Susan Fisher, and I was startled when she was offended by it. I thought it was just a friendly little word like rascal, but Susy explained to me that a momser is someone whose parents are closely related, and it really is a terribly derogatory term.

Only today (Sept. 16, 1983) I discovered the meaning of a Yiddish phrase that was used often in my childhood environment; "A Chali-aliah zulla choppen." At Dr. Goldenberg's office I learned that "Chali-aliah" is cholera, and it means, "May you be grabbed by cholera." Pretty strong eh?

# WHY GE HIRED ME

Some time before my last year in college I became obsessed with the idea of working for a large company, and in particular General Electric. I'm not sure I know why, except General Electric had something called a "Creative Engineering Course," that seemed to me like a marvelous thing for a young engineer to attend, and a way up the ladder into doing creative, inventive things.

I think it was in the first half of my last year that I took a course in internal combustion engines with Professor Kent. He was a stuffy, WASP type guy who gave a course that was noted for its difficulty, but was required for all mechanical engineering students. When we got to the mid-term exam in the course, some of us conceived the idea of looking carefully at his previous final exams for clues about his favorite type of questions. The Mechanical Engineering Dept. kept, and made available to the students, a file of final exams that had been given by all the teachers. We went over his exams and made the startling discovery that all the problems that he gave were really the same problem. It was a particular type of thermodynamic problem. There were 5 variables with a complex mathematical relation among them having to do with the CARNOT Cycle. He would give you 4 of them and ask for the fifth. He would vary which four he gave you, but the relationship was the same. Three or four of us recognized this fact and we worked together on these problems and discovered how to do them quickly; how to handle the slide rule; and how to recognize which factors were the input and which were required as the answer. We got pretty good at it and did very well on the mid-term. In fact, we averaged in the nineties, while the rest of the class averaged in the forties.

After that there was another exam and all of the problems were the same classic problem, but in one of them two of the

Inputs were missing, so you couldn't do the problem. Professor Kent was proctoring the exam himself. I walked up to the front of the room and said to him quietly that there wasn't enough information there to do the seventh problem. He looked it over and told me that there was enough information. I sat down, looked at it again, and decided that there really wasn't, so I just didn't do anything on that problem. Maybe I wrote that there wasn't enough information given.

When the exams came back I got a zero on that question, and any of the other students who had fumbled around with it without knowing what they were doing, got full credit. I thought chat was awful, and I went to talk with him about it afterwards. He brushed me aside and wouldn't hear anything about it. He said I hadn't even tried, and he would have given me full credit if I had written anything down in an attempt to solve the problem. I reminded him that I had told him during the exam that there wasn't enough information there to do the problem, but he brushed that aside too. I decided to take my lumps and do nothing about it.

By the time of the final exam, most of the students recognized that some of us had something going that they didn't know anything about. They inquired, and we ended up holding classes on how to do what we called "Professor Kent's Problem." The whole class got very good grades.

When we came to the Interviews for jobs, GE interviewed me and subsequently hired me. I looked at a list of the people they interviewed. There were only three; the guy at the top of the class, number two in the class and me. I was probably about a third of the way down. I marveled that they should pick me for the interview, and then I discovered that they relied on Professor Kent to pick the students that they were going to interview. I guess he clearly understood what had happened with that question I got a zero on. He couldn't back up, but felt guilty about it.

Sometimes I think how much that influenced my life. After I worked for GE for about a year, they had some sort of arrangement with NOL that involved transferring the engineers for whom they couldn't get draft exemptions to the Naval Ordnance Laboratory, where they would be inducted into The Navy and continue working as ordnance engineers. I was one of the people transferred, and that's how I came to work for NOL. NOL did, in fact, get me inducted into the Navy when I was drafted, and I became Chief Specialist Miscellaneous. I worked on torpedoes and mines all during the war at The Naval Gun Factory. The first night I spent away from home was the night I was discharged from The Navy.

That reminds me that someplace among my papers is an article which my Aunt Jeanette wrote for a law journal, I think, entitled, "Don't Tell Him Off." I remember reading that article and thinking about the Professor Kent story at that time.

In passing the subject, there's another memory about job interviews in college. Generally you had to make application for an interview and answer questions. One of the questions on one of the applications for Mechanical Engineers was whether you liked to work with small delicate things or large rugged devices. All the students liked to work on large rugged devices. Now you might consider this odd except that the application was for an interview with the Mack Truck Company.

# LIEUTENANT J.G. G.J. HALL

I was inducted into The Navy, through my draft board, sometime in late 1944, and became an instant chief. At that time I had already been transferred to The Naval Ordnance Laboratory, where I was working as a civilian engineer. All of us engineers who were draft bait either became ensigns or chiefs. Mostly the reason for being a chief instead of an ensign was some physical disability, usually eyes. There was nothing wrong with my eyes, and I don't know why I was refused a commission, although I suspect it was because I had written the wrong answer on an application to the question of my drinking habits. I wrote that I didn't drink at all, and I think The Navy didn't like that. They preferred people who drank occasionally or socially or something like that. I did, in fact, drink on occasion, and I don't know why I answered the question that way. At any rate, there was no recourse, and I was a chief. The pay and allowances all came to about the same thing, whether you were a chief, an ensign, or a P-1 (lowest civil service level) engineer, which I had been before.

There were just three things I recall that distinguished being in The Navy from being a civilian engineer, although the work was the same. I wore a uniform; I had to take guard duty about once every two weeks; and we had drill on Friday afternoons. This story has to do mostly with the Friday afternoon drill.

My first meeting with Lieutenant J.G. G.J. Hall was when I went to complain about being given guard duty on Christmas Eve. I thought that was unfair. I went into his office to complain about it. He looked up at me quietly and said, "You took two days off for the Jewish holidays, didn't you?"

Of course there was no arguing with that. He was right. I simply thanked him for his time and took my guard duty.

My second experience has to do with the drill. We were at The Gun Factory in Washington. At that time I think it was called The Washington Navy Yard. They had a big square called a quadrangle in which we chiefs would drill for an hour every Friday afternoon. Lieutenant Hall was the drill master, and we would all line up and march: right face, left fact, about face. A hundred or so marines would ring the field and snicker. We were indeed a very sloppy bunch. As a matter of fact, we giggled a good deal ourselves. On one occasion, when I was laughing pretty hard, Lieutenant Hall called me over and said, "Alright, smarty, let's see you call the drill."

It looked easy enough. So he stepped back out of the way, and I started out with 16 chiefs, 4 abreast in 4 rows, and I started calling, "Forward march, left right, to the rear," and things like that. Now it turns out there's some skill required. You have to call at the right point or people get confused about whether they're on one step or the next. Presently I had my 16 chiefs strung out and laughing so hard they couldn't march. They were in rows of 2 and 3, with spaces in between, and a few of them were on the other side of the drill field. The marines were roaring. Lieutenant Hall was splitting his sides, and everybody was having a jolly good time at my embarrassment.

My next encounter with Lieutenant Hall was when I shot the hole in the guard trailer. That was really the mark of distinction in my Navy career. When we had overnight guard duty, they would issue us a pistol in a holster with instructions not to take it out. Of course, that is not something that a spirited young man could resist; so I took the pistol out one night and was playing with it. I was pointing it at the water spigot inside the watch trailer, which was essentially a house trailer. I was sitting on a bench in the kitchen, pointing it at the sink spigot. I would put it on the empty chamber and pull the trigger. Well, one time it wasn't on the empty chamber. I must say, I hit the spigot. The bullet split into two parts and went out of the trailer.

I wrote in the log that I had discharged the pistol. I spent the rest of the night wondering what on earth they were going to do to me. There was an ensign in charge of the watch, and he showed up to relieve me in the morning. I told him the story. His immediate idea was to put another bullet in the gun and say nothing about it; if he could find another bullet. I told him I had entered it in the log, whereupon he took me to see Lieutenant J.G. G.J. Hall. I needed a shave. I was tired and had been up all night. I felt like a bum. I was depressed, and Lieutenant Hall was absolutely horrified. He could see immediately that this thing was beyond him. He therefore took me to see Lieutenant Commander Ethridge, who also thought that this was quite beyond him, and we went to see Commander Sellers, a great senior naval officer.

Commander Sellers was busy, and we waited in his office for about an hour and a half while he saw other people and took care of more urgent business. Finally we got in to see him; me, the ensign in charge of the watch, the Lieutenant Commander, and Lieutenant J.G. G.J. Hall. Between them they started to explain what had happened. The essence of the story was very simple. Commander Sellers listened patiently, and his reaction was, "What are you bothering me with this trivia for? Give him some extra guard duty and go away."

That was the end of the story. The only lasting effect was that for months after that, when I rode in the bus to work or back, I would often see people pointing me out to each other in the bus and whispering. I knew that I was being identified as the celebrity who shot the hole in the trailer.

Needless to say, I had a lot of extra guard duty. But it really wasn't so bad. I felt truly contrite anyhow. The war ended that year, and I was discharged from the Navy shortly afterwards at the convenience of the government. At that point I had a choice of whether to go back to GE or remain with The Naval Ordnance Laboratory. In view of the fact that Lillian put her foot down about going back to Schenectady; that was something she absolutely was completely loathe to do, I remained at The Naval Ordnance Laboratory in Washington.

That was the only time in our married life that Lillian was that firm about my career. Later when I left the government to start my own business and I fully expected her to protest vigorously, she just said, "Well if that's what you want to do..."

# MISCELLANEOUS COLLEGE MEMORIES

Shortly before I came to City College, the president was a staunch conservative named Frederick Robinson, and the student body was very radical. A very strong conflict ensued, the result of which was that a number of the college agitators were suspended, expelled, etc. Of course these radicals, as usual, tended to be leaders and very good students. As a result of that, the college newspaper, named The Campus, carried at its masthead the following legend, "The College of The City of New York, Famous for the Caliber of The Men It Expels."

I came into the college intending to major in Physics, but switched to mechanical engineering. Years later in graduate school I went back to physics. I was out of school for, I think, 6 months, working as a machinist. My grades during my first year in school were rather poor and I was on a C probation, which meant that I could not take more than 12 credits. I remember that I was accused during that time of majoring in ping pong.

Occasionally, when I had no early classes, I would walk to the college from home. We lived on the Bronx side of The Washington Bridge, and I walked over High Bridge and through the parks along the river bank. It was a very pleasant walk, mostly through parkland. Today that's a walk no white person would ever dare to make. It may even have been risky in those days, but I didn't know it.

There was a well equipped machine shop at the college for the use of the Mechanical Engineers, but there were no courses given in shop, and it was not used. Years later I recognized that as part of the "upgraded curriculum" syndrome, shop courses turn into courses in metallurgy, and brick laying turns into ceramics. Similarly the trade school Andrew Carnegie founded turned into Carnegie Mellon University. I think it's the faculty that is the prime mover in this evolutionary process.

Some of the students were very poor, and one of my friends, Enoch Dubinski, frequently lunched on mayonnaise. He would go through the cafeteria line, pick up a saucer, and take it past the cashier heaped with mayonnaise. Since it was a condiment, it was free. We all agreed in a philosophical discussion that that was not dishonest if one could stand a lunch of nothing but mayonnaise. Presently, however, Enoch took to putting a slice of white bread on the saucer before heaping on enough mayonnaise to hide it. That was stealing. The bread sold for 2c a slice.

The lunchroom consisted of a large central open space surrounded by "alcoves." Each alcove had a large table about 4 ft by 8 ft with benches fixed to the walls on 3 sides of it. The 4th side opened into the central area. Nobody ate on those benches. It was clearly understood by all that they were strictly for ping pong, and indeed, between 10 AM and 2 PM there was a ping pong game going on on every one of them with people on the benches watching and waiting their turns.

# LENNY ACROSS-THE-STREET

When my friend Al Wadman was a boy he took piano lessons, and, like so many kids, he was not very dedicated. However, there was a kid across the street named Lenny who was always held up to him as the shining example. They could often hear him practicing, and Al's mother would say, "Why aren't you practicing like Lenny across-the-street?"; or "Let me hear you play the piano like Lenny across-the-street"; or "Listen to Lenny across-the-street! Why can't you play like him?"

Lenny's last name was Bernstein: **THE** Leonard Bernstein.

# LILRAFF

Al Wadman rode, kept and bred Arabian riding horses. The greatest of the Arabian horses was named Raffles, and to show descent from him, horse breeders liked to put Raff in their horses' names, like Raffmead or Raffson. Al had a filly descended from Raffles, and with Lil's permission, he named her Lilraff. Later he had a colt that he named Samraff. Before I gave permission, I made him promise that Samraff would not be gelded.

# RECITING

In the twenties, at least in the Jewish community in The Bronx, each child was supposed to have some special ability to show off, either singing or dancing or reciting. In my case it was reciting. At children's parties, and sometimes even at family gatherings, the children would be called upon to do their little thing. I remember it particularly as a feature of kid's birthday parties. We would play pin the tail on the donkey and things like that, but then there would be some part of the time when each kid was called upon to do his act. At this time the parents stood around and "kvelled."

I don't remember any particular birthday parties, although I do remember some of the poems that I used to do. One of them, which I recaptured recently into my memory was called "Johnny's Hist'ry Lesson." Audrey Platt found it for me in a book. I doubt if I did the whole thing, but I remember my mother helping me with the expression and emotion in it. I also did one about "I stood on the bridge at midnight and the clock was striking the hour." That was an imitation of a class recitation where you imitated different accents as you went through it. There was the Italian boy, the Jewish boy, the bashful boy, a boy who stuttered, and you finally ended up with the boy who wanted to be an actor and the boy who didn't care. There was also a piece called "Baths" of which the outstanding line was, "What are baths for anyhow? You take one and then you have to take another."

My most vivid recollection of reciting did not have to do with parties, but reciting at home when my mother's family was there. The piece I used to recite most often, on request, was "Mother of Mine."

It was what we would call today a very schmaltzy piece. It started out, "Radiant, beautiful, wonderful, gifted with treasures rare, more than all riches of mankind, may God protect and spare." It was my Uncle Harry who used to request that piece, and he would cry when I would recite it. He would cry real honest tears. That may have been during the period shortly after my grandmother, his mother, had died. In any case, I remember this mixed feeling of power and embarrassment that by reciting that piece I could make a grown man cry.

There are two other recitation occasions which I find in my memory. One was at some sort of event at Camp Shari, the only camp I ever went to as a child, and I don't think I spent a whole summer there. They had some sort of a kiddie contest at which I recited. It is perhaps indicative of the cultural milieu that I always thought Shari was some kind of an Indian name, while it is actually the Hebrew word for welcome.

I recited a poem that was taught to me by some of the counselors. Sylvia was a counselor at the time, and I think she was one of those involved. It goes like this:

"Jack and Jill went up the hill to fetch a pail of water. Jill came down with a five dollar bill. Do you think she went after water?"

With no understanding of the content of the poem, I brought down the house and won the contest.

The other occasion is one I shall always file away as my most embarrassing moment. I recited a poem in the school auditorium. I think it must have been in public school; but before several hundred children. The poem was one by Robert W. Service entitled "Fleurette." I did that once, and it was a great hit. About a year later they asked me to do it again. I can't recall now whether I was asked suddenly because something else that was supposed to be on the program wasn't there, or whether I actually did have time to review it, but didn't. In any case, I started gallantly into this poem and there was something in the fourth stanza that led me back into the second stanza. So I went through the second stanza, the third stanza and the beginning of the fourth stanza again; with less confidence. When I got to the middle of the fourth stanza, lo and behold! I was back at the beginning of the second stanza again. I went through the 2nd stanza, the 3rd stanza, the beginning of the fourth stanza and I was back in the second stanza again. I couldn't seem to get out of it. There was some tittering from the kids in the auditorium, who by this time recognized that they were hearing the same words over and over again, and finally I bowed and sat down. I think that at the time I quit I was going through the third stanza for the fourth time.

# THE GREAT DRUG STORE SWINDLE

At some time, probably while I was in public school, I had a part time job delivering for Bergman's Drug Store. The drug store was on Featherbed Lane, and I would deliver prescriptions. People sometimes would pay me, and I carried change.

On one occasion a man stopped me in the street and asked if I worked for Bergman's Drug Store. He explained that he owed Bergman's some money, and that if I would come with him, he would give it to me. We went into the lobby of an apartment house. Somehow he had a ten dollar bill, for which I had change. He took the change and went up to his apartment to get the ten dollar bill. After he didn't come back, I went up to the apartment and they had never heard of him. Among other things, I realized that I couldn't even describe the man. God! I felt stupid!

This, of course, was a disaster to me. Ten dollars was an awful lot of money in those days. He had taken most of that from me. My father went and discussed it with Bergman, and they arranged somehow to split the loss. My father comforted me by telling me that I was lucky that I was swindled while I was still very young and there wasn't much money involved. I had learned a lesson very cheap. Then he proceeded to tell me many stories about friends of his that had been swindled, and they were really marvelous stories. I was in a very agitated state, but they calmed me down and I really enjoyed listening to him. It was one of the most pleasant times that I spent with my father. Not that any of the times I spent with my father were unpleasant, but I just don't remember that much closeness on many other occasions.

The stories he told were really marvelous. All sorts of grifting stories, including the dropped package, the printing press that made dollar bills, and several different varieties of "switch grifting."

At some time later in life I remember being involved with a man who sold French postcards on 42nd Street. That was a moderately amusing situation. There were several of us there in our late teens, and he sort of slid up to us, looking furtively around, and explained that he had some very nice French postcards. He wasn't allowed to sell them, but he could give them away. He would sell us a chocolate bar, a 10c chocolate bar for a dollar, and he would give us the stack of postcards. Well, that seemed like a pretty good deal, so we bought the chocolate bar and he gave us the stack of post cards. They were pictures of The Louvre, The Eiffel Tower, The Seine River; not at all what we expected. We found him, a few minutes later, further down the street looking for another patsy, and we protested that those were not what we expected. He reminded us that he had given it to us free. He'd only sold us the chocolate bar. Was the chocolate bar what we expected?

# MY DAY IN JAIL

I actually spent a day in jail. There were four of us. We were in college. We had gone down to Manhattan on some sort of a holiday and rented bicycles from a bicycle shop near Central Park, and were riding through the park. We came down a long walk and saw a policeman at the bottom. He was waving to us to go back. We ignored him and continued on down the path. When we got to the bottom, he stopped us and explained very politely that we shouldn't be riding bicycles on that walk. Our leader at the time was a fellow student named Herbie Lehr, whose father was a lawyer. Herbie fancied himself something of a legal expert too. He immediately took over the discussion with the police officer. It went something like this: "You kids shouldn't be riding bicycles here; it's a walk."

"Why not?"

"You might knock somebody down."

"We'll be careful."

"It's a sidewalk. Would you ride a bicycle on the sidewalk in front of your own house?"

"I do it every day."

"Would you ride a bicycle on the sidewalk at 42nd Street and Times Square?"

"I might or I might not, but if I wanted to, you couldn't stop me."

That, as I recall, was the end of the discussion. After that we all had to produce identification, and we got traffic tickets. We were required to appear in court about 2 weeks later. The charge was driving a vehicle on the sidewalk.

When our great moment came; our turn at justice, Herbie cleared his throat and rose to speak. "First of all, your honor, it was not a vehicle, it was a bicycle."

The judge interrupted abruptly with, "A bicycle is a vehicle. One dollar fine."

"I won't pay it!"

"A day in Jail."

There was nothing for us but to join him. That was our loyalty. Besides that, by this time we already knew that a day in jail ended at 3 in the afternoon, and it was now about 11 in the morning. That was only about 4 hours. Twenty-five cents an hour was pretty good wages for doing nothing, so we did, in fact, spend the time in jail.

It was really a rather amusing experience. We met all sorts of hardened criminals; mostly street vendors without licenses. One in particular was a very amusing fellow who sold five dollar bills, two for a quarter. The five dollar bills were clearly marked phony all over them, but he had a wonderful spiel that went with it. People would buy the bills just for the amusement of listening to his spiel, which had parts in it like, "Take these five dollar bills into any bank in the country and they'll give you five singles for it. I guarantee it, but you have to do it right. You have to have two friends standing in the doorway; big tough guys, armed."

The jailor was a really nice kind of guy, and he recognized that we were college kids and probably wouldn't eat the prison lunch. So he said that if one of us would leave something for security, he could go out and bring in lunch for the others. I volunteered and left my raincoat. As long as I was out, I passed a barber shop and got a haircut before I brought in the sandwiches. Unfortunately the jailor noticed that I got a haircut, and he was indignant. He felt that I had taken advantage of his good graces. I had hoped he wouldn't notice.

Many years later I came across Herbie Lehr's name again. He was personnel director at The Brookhaven National Laboratory. I verified that it was him by the name, age, and the fact that he was a City College graduate, but he was not in the day I was there, so I never got a chance to talk to him, and to remind him of that auspicious beginning for his abortive legal career.

# A EULOGY I DELIVERED AT EDMUND TROUNSON'S FUNERAL IN THE SUMMER OF 83

I'm not sure what I'm supposed to do up here. Tom Phipps has prepared a magnificent eulogy for Ed, which you have in your hands. Ed's pictures out there speak volumes about him, and in a very important sense, they are part of him; living on amongst us. Some of them will be on display at The Smithsonian Summer Folk Festival at the end of this month and the beginning of July. That's quite a tribute too. So I'm Just going to tell a few stories that have been rattling around in the back of my head for decades. It's thoroughly in keeping with Ed's spirit not to care what I'm supposed to say up here.

As a young engineer I came to work at The Naval Ordnance Laboratory almost 40 years ago and Ed was my boss for about 10 years. He was more than my boss. He and I and a few others were a close knit social group that rallied round several times a week. We usually rallied at my house because I was the only one who was married. I recall one night after dinner we all went to a movie and when we came back for ice cream, Ed picked up the paper and found that "The Lady Vanishes" was playing at another local theater and there was still time to make the late show. The force of his character and enthusiasm was such that we all had to gobble up our ice cream and dash off to another movie. That story always stuck in my mind, and I'll come back to it later.

Ed had a relationship to science like Abraham had to God in Genesis. Abraham asked questions and God answered them. Of course Ed's questions were in the form of experiments - simple clever experiments.

There was a problem with premature firing of proximity fuses and Ed decided that it could be due to near field antenna sensitivity. He made a little wax paper cone which he simply stuck over the nose of the fuse while we observed its behavior. He was right, and the experiment proved his point. The engineers of Eastman Kodak, who made the fuses, had a much more complicated explanation of the prematuring and there was a shoot-out; a sort of scientific confrontation between Ed and four learned Kodak scientists. It was David and Goliath. He slew them all with the piece of wax paper. In later years Al Wadman and others referred to that as the "ham sandwich wrapper experiment," and some of you may have heard of it.

I recall that in the relaxed atmosphere at NOL right after the war ended, he was curious about the behavior of beetles. They seemed to go in circles aimlessly. Did they know where they were going? Were they heading out or heading home or just wandering. He got a stick and a bucket of tar and followed one for hours one afternoon, putting drops of tar behind it. Presently he could see that the tar spots formed a lovely spiral track and the beetle did have a direction. It was making progress in a constant direction although it seemed to be going in circles.

I remember too how he measured the charge on raindrops. He put a sheet of tin out in the rain and ran a wire to an oscilloscope inside the lab and watched the pulses when the drops hit.

Music fascinated him. We went out together to the atomic bomb tests in Bikini - in those days Bikini was not yet a bathing suit - It was a small ring of islands near the equator in mid-Pacific where the Navy did a series of bomb tests. We were part of the test group and he persuaded me to bring an ochorina. He bought a flagelette and we would try to play simple tunes together at night on the fantail of The USS Wharton. We were awful! But he had the most wonderful theories about harmony and tone combinations that were pleasing to the ear, and how you could get your voice to resonate with machinery and motor boats, and even about how tolerant people should be of embryonic musicians.

While we were there he showed me the snails coming up to the sea cucumbers on the coral reefs and staying quite still while the sea cucumbers cleaned the algae off their shells. That was my first introduction to what is called today cleaning symbiosis.

Charlotte told me the story of his buying the house on Notley Road. He looked at the main floor and the basement and announced that he would buy it without even seeing the upstairs. I have no doubt about that because he once explained to me his theory of how to buy a house. The important thing is the people you buy it from. If they are honest, clean and industrious, you'll get a good buy and you don't have to see the whole house to know that. One or two observations in the basement will tell the whole story.

I promised to come back to the movie "The Lady Vanishes." I hadn't seen much of Ed in several years - I don't know why - I guess we were both busy with other things; and a few months ago I noticed at the public library that they were going to show "The Lady Vanishes" at that same library next Saturday afternoon. I thought that would be a great opportunity for a nostalgic reunion and I called him. He was in the hospital and I later talked to him on the phone. All he wanted to talk about was the lubrication experiments he was doing — and they are fascinating. He had discovered electrical phenomena going on in lubricants as they work, and he was beginning to understand them with a bunch of typical Ed Trounson simple, elegant experiments — measuring the voltage across spinning bearings and the effect of speed and film thickness and surface roughness. As usual, his ideas were fascinating, and I asked all sorts of detailed questions, but not about how he was feeling. After about half an hour of this he apologized abruptly. "I have to hang up now, there's a doctor on one side of my bed with a shot in his hand and a nurse on the other side who is threatening to grab the phone. I have all these tubes sticking in me and they have to change something or other. Call back soon."

The first three times I visited him in the hospice, and I must digress a moment to comment about the beautiful people who took care of him there. There he was not the patient in 1A1B. He was Mr. Trounson, spelled out in an elegant wood grained plaque, and the people there really cared about him and about his visitors. In these visits I learned about Chaucer. Ed had found another fascinating subject for his probing mind. I learned among other things that there are two inventions of Chaucer's time that are still with us — from the 14th century. Do you know what they are — the mechanical clock and the pencil — the wooden pencil! Someone invented it in the 14th century. What enormous implications for trade and literacy. A person no longer had to have a goose quill pen and a pot of ink. He could just pull a pencil out of his pocket and make a notation or do a sum or send a message. Those are the kinds of things Ed liked to talk about and think about and learn about. In the time we shared together I caught some of it from him, and I am sure grateful.

If you've never heard the story of Ed's first trip to Europe, you should at least know that he went with no luggage. Just a lot of photographic equipment hung around his neck and what he could carry in his pockets. Someone, maybe Mrs. Modine, sewed special additional pockets inside his jacket. I have a little vignette of custom officials standing with stickers in hand saying incredulously, "No luggage?" Who else but our beloved Ed Trounson?

Another thing I learned from Ed during his last days was that Frederick II of Naples in twelve hundred and something discovered the migration of birds. He was a scientist with great material resources (being a King), and he sent people out to observe. Before him they believed that birds came from clams. That's not so strange a belief when you consider that they had found other flying things coming from caterpillars and worms.

Don't expect me to sum all this up or draw any conclusions. I'm nowhere near smart enough for that. I would like to close by reading a letter from Steve Lee. Steve is the son of Charlie Lee who was one of that close knit social group that used to rally round for dinner 40 years ago — dinner and movies.

— End of Eulogy —

I'm sorry I didn't keep a copy of the letter. It's about how Steve's son enjoyed Ed's visits just like Steve did when he was little; the clever games and the toys Ed would make for him.

# THE GREAT DEPRESSION

I don't remember the great depression particularly as an event. It came on and departed so gradually that when we were in it, it just seemed to me that that's the way things always were. On my way to high school I walked over The Washington Bridge. That's the bridge that goes from The Bronx into Manhattan and ends up at 181st Street in Manhattan. I used to go over it almost every day, and as you walked over the bridge before you got to the river, you could look down on The Bronx side into what I later learned was called a "Hoovertown." It was a collection of makeshift shelters, the best of which were packing crates covered with tarpaper. Signs of various types were used in the construction, that is, billboards and things like that. One shack tended to be leaning up against another, possibly because they only had one wall between them. There were little garden plots around them, and fires were lit in the winter. That was public land, and afterwards it became a park. I guess it may have been a park then, but people were squatting on it. I never recognized that as a product of depression. That was just a town where very poor people lived. It seemed to me that it had always been that way and always would be. My Uncle Jack, who was the husband of my mother's sister Tess (who Terri is named after), drove a cab during that period, and at one time his cab was in an accident and destroyed. He had no way of making a living. So, as people did in those days before there was welfare and public handouts, he turned to his family. None of us had very much, but I remember that Eddie and Sylvia and I all had bank accounts where we put savings from our allowance and earnings of various types.

Usually when we put this money away, my father would match it or exceed it; so that it was really his money, but the bank accounts were in our names. I recall that we cleaned out our bank accounts to get the money together so Jack could buy a new cab. Sylvia had the most money, which was something over a hundred dollars. It seems to me that I had $40, and Eddie must have had something in between. This was not done by our parents without our cooperation. I remember that it was discussed with us. Jack needed a cab, and we were in a position to help him, and we all gave wholeheartedly of course. Later on Jack had somehow gotten into the meat business and was doing reasonably well, or at least his wife, Tess, who I loved dearly, was doing well in the meat business, and Jack was doing something useful. My father's business collapsed, and he needed $500 to go into another business. Jack lent him the money.

It seems to me in retrospect that one of the things that the depression did was to bring families much closer together. They had to rely on each other, as there was no one else to rely on. Your family was what you really had in those days.

Outside of that event with Uncle Jack and his taxicab, I was pretty well shielded from the depression by my parents. I know there must have been times when there was no money, or almost no money for food, and no idea where the next money was coming from. I know that my father gave up his place of business downtown, and that was one of the reasons we moved out of that apartment house. He was obsessed with the idea of renting part of a two or three family house which had a basement, which he could use for what was left of his business. We did it and it must have worked. We all helped him during that period, particularly Eddie and me.

In the late twenties my father was the king of the hard rubber comb business, and hard rubber combs were the only kind worth having. Plastic combs broke when you used them. He sold principally under the name of Gotham.

But the plastic combs got better and cheaper, and some time around 1934 my father had to start making them. The principal expense was the mold and he invested in one. Within a few months the competition was selling combs cheaper than he could make them — because they had a multiple mold that made four combs at one time. He invested in a four comb mold and was soon grossly under priced again because someone was molding twelve at a time. So it went until there were only two companies struggling for dominance in the market; my father and DuPont. DuPont won and my father went into reselling — jobbing it was called — and that's when he moved his shop into the basement at 1624 Nelson Avenue.

I particularly remember putting clips on combs in that basement. They were metal clips like those on fountain pens, to hold them in your pocket. I drilled holes in the fat part of the comb, pushed the clips in and hammered over the prongs. I also remember packing combs in boxes and boxes in cartons. I remember being reprimanded for not completely removing a label from a carton we were reusing. It was a carton in which the combs had been shipped to us. If the customer could read the label, he'd know where we bought them and could go there and buy them himself, cheaper. Jobbing is a strange business. My father tried everything to make a living in those days. I even remember shipping condoms from that basement. The $500 from my Uncle Jack, as I recall, was to put my father in the pants business. I think he had a partner who knew something about pants, but I think the partner "sold him a bill of goods;" which was one of my father's favorite expressions. Finally he hooked up with a lawyer named Elkins back in the comb business. Elkins knew nothing about combs, but he had capital. Together they weathered the rest of the depression. Eddie worked for them too, despite frequent run-ins with Elkins, and even with my father.

# CHARLIE CHARLES

I think his middle name was Charles too. He was a close friend of my father who loved to tell very dirty jokes. I was old enough at that time to at least recognize, if not to appreciate dirty jokes. We visited and vacationed with his family a lot.

At one time when he owned a restaurant in downtown New York, my father and I stopped in to visit him late one morning and we chatted. When lunchtime came he took us across the street for lunch. I asked him why we didn't eat in his restaurant.

"Don't tell anyone kid, but my cook spits in the soup." Then as an afterthought, "Maybe the cook spits in the soup here too, but at least I don't see him doing it."

# BREADED VEAL CUTLETS

The first time I had dinner at Lillian's house, when we were courting, it was a pleasant polite experience. Her mother made breaded veal cutlets. I suppose I said and did all the right things. The next time I had dinner at her house we had breaded veal cutlets again. The third time I said to Lillian, "Doesn't your mother know how to make anything but breaded veal cutlets?"

Her somewhat frosty and emphatic reply was, "My mother thinks you are crazy about veal cutlets."

Maybe I was too polite.

# A VERSE I WROTE FOR
# LILLIAN ABOUT 1950

Suppose that I could start again;
Beyond the real world's border
Where things were so contrived for men
That wives were made to order.
I would not order me a Queen,
For queens are much too haughty
And angels don't suit my demean,
For they are never naughty.
A bustling home adoring wife
Eventually would bore me.
A genius at my side for life
Would surely overawe me.
So I'd have one made with all your ways
To the last minute maneuver;
And marry her and spend my days
Attempting to improve her.

# LILLIAN

We used to tell people that we met in a bathroom, but that was not exactly right. Actually the bathroom scene was very important in our relationship, but we had been introduced before that. It was at a party at Chez Karl, which I'll tell you about later. I had gotten very high at this party, and had gone into the bathroom to splash cold water on my face. Before doing that I had the good sense to take off my shirt and undershirt. So I was stripped to the waist, splashing cold water on my face, when the door opened (I think it opened in, actually), and Lillian took a step forward. I had, of course, not locked the door. I was drunk enough to grab her and kiss her, getting her somewhat wet at the time. But she accepted it with good grace, and I hope, even with some enjoyment. That was the moment we always referred to when we said we met in a bathroom.

Karl Kramer was Lillian's cousin, and it was through him that I met Lillian. Just to get the family relationship straight, Martin Buckner had a sister named Esther, and Karl was her only child. He was an awkward sort of guy, the kind we would call a klutz. He walked up to me one day in the schoolyard and announced that he intended to be my friend. He did, in fact, become my friend, and he was a member of the Alpha Phi Pi fraternity, ultimately; along with Julie Rubin, Myron Joseph, Joe Baumowitz, (later Joe Baum), Al Post and Eddie Goldstone. However he didn't hang on as long as the rest of them, and I really don't know what became of him. I think he moved to California.

To return to the story, Karl was my friend, Lillian was his cousin, and he offered to introduce me to her (or her to me). He explained to her beforehand though that, "Sam is not the marrying kind." Lillian replied, "We'll see about that." And indeed she did.

I think Karl brought her to that party specifically to meet me. I know I didn't have a date, and I took her home afterwards.

At that time Karl had another friend named Carl Chase, and they lived together in a little apartment in downtown New York, which explains the name they used for the apartment. They had a lot of crazy parties there. I specifically remember one in which we were all sitting on the floor telling ghost stories, and the only way they could arrange appropriate lighting for the event was to turn all the lights off and leave the refrigerator door open.

We were married after a delightful, sexy, long courtship. It was the weekend after I graduated from college. I remember we stopped making love, by mutual agreement, two or three weeks before the wedding, so that we wouldn't take all the excitement out of our wedding night.

Lillian's sister, Rosalind, told me several times that she has one very distinct memory of our wedding, which was that my brother Eddie brought his dog on a leash. My recollection about my brother Eddie and the wedding was a little different. I remember that he was my best man, and we came to the hall together in a hurry, a little bit late. In the street outside a man asked him if he knew how to fix a camera, which the man was having trouble with, and my brother stopped, and I had to wait while he fumbled with that poor fellow's camera. My recollection is that his wife Claire (they were already married) brought the dog. To prove that I am right, the dog's name was Miss T, so named because she had done a lot of traveling. "T" was short for Traveler.

The wedding was in the afternoon of September 24, 1943. We spent our wedding night at my father's bungalow in Lake Mohegan. By then his business affairs had recovered to the point where he had a summer bungalow. Lillian and I had worked to build a fireplace in it. We dug the footing and poured some rocks and cement in, but my father had it finished professionally, although he always referred to it as the fireplace Lillian and I built.

It was a brisk late September evening and that fireplace was all the heat we had; and romantic too, so we lit a fire and slept in the living room. The only sleep-able furniture in that room, however, was a 20 inch wide chair that folded out into a 20 Inch wide bed with the chair arms up against the bed on both sides. We made love and slept in it. That was togetherness! It reminds me of the time we took Anna Buckner camping with us in California (one night only) about 11 years later. There was one sleeping bag each for Mel, Brian, Anna, and one left over for Lillian and me. Of course there was no sex that night, and very little sleep either. When you get two bodies in a single sleeping bag — oh boy!

We honeymooned in The Pocono Mountains. I can't remember the name of the hotel. Someplace during the honeymoon we went horseback riding, and I was thrown. It was a little narrow trail along the edge of a cliff, and Lillian was up ahead of me. I had a skittish horse, but it was a rather brisk morning, so I had laid the reins down on the saddle and put my hands in my pockets to keep warm. A chipmunk ran across the path in front of the horse, and he took off. My recollection of my fall is that I was still sitting there, but the horse was gone. Fortunately it was one of the few wide gravelly places on the trail. When my horse caught up to Lillian, which he did in a few dozen steps, the trail had again narrowed with a steep cliff on one side and a steep fall-off on the other. When she looked around and saw the empty saddle, she thought she was already a widow. The damage, however, was a badly scraped hip. In fact, the skin was scraped over a length of about 9 inches, and 3 inches of width. When we got back to the hotel, my new bride thought the proper treatment was to put peroxide on it. I had to keep from screaming to show my manliness, but it wasn't easy.

After the honeymoon I went back to college to make sure I had passed all my courses. I discovered the close call in my Civil Engineering class (see "Cheating in College"), and we set off to Schenectady to start our married life together. We didn't have a car at that time. I had borrowed either Martin Buckner's car or my father's car for the honeymoon. I remember that Martin Buckner went to great travail to get us gas stamps, because it was wartime. At any rate, after the honeymoon we went to Schenectady by train.

When we arrived at the train station, we had no hotel reservations or anyplace to go, so we just got into a cab and asked the driver to take us to a good hotel. It turns out that there were two hotels in Schenectady at that time: the good one and the bad one. The good one was the Van Curler. We went to The Mohawk at the recommendation of the cab driver. Because it was wartime, you couldn't get a cab by yourself. It was a group of 5. Well, we spent about 45 minutes in that cab, riding around and dropping off passengers. We were the last ones. I don't recall what the cab fare was, but it was substantial. We were finally at The Mohawk Hotel. It was rather noisy, but otherwise okay. In the morning, when we went out of the hotel, as I stuck my head out the door, I could see the railroad station down the street. Boy, were we taken!

Most of the time we lived in Schenectady, we lived in a furnished apartment, which was half a floor in a three floor house. We had the front half of the middle floor, which consisted of a bedroom just large enough for a double bed and a chair, a huge kitchen, a large living room, and a walk-through closet. You walked through it to get to the porch, which was out front. The apartment didn't have a bathroom, but there was a bath on our floor which was used by us and the other apartment which was the back of the same floor. The bath had two doors to it, one to our apartment and one to theirs. The first couple we shared the bathroom with was named Wood. I recall because his name was Gar Wood, a famous name in racing I believe, but he was not related to the famous Gar Wood. We had very little to do with them, but Lillian was perpetually annoyed with the fact that he would apparently sit on the toilet and flick his cigarette ashes into the bathtub without cleaning them out before he left.

The second couple we shared that bathroom with was Lenny and Shirley Brenner, with whom I am still friendly. They now live in Washington. We were very friendly with them then, and it was not uncommon for us to leave both bathroom doors open so that we could visit with each other by walking through the bathroom.

Most of the time we were in Schenectady, Lillian worked for General Electric on the day shift, and I worked the graveyard shift, which was from about 11 at night to 7 in the morning. She slept alone, except for weekends. One night she was awakened because of a pressure on her chest. When she opened her eyes, there was a pair of eyes looking into hers. She afterwards recalled that as one of the greatest frights of her life. What happened was that the doors to the bathroom were open; the Brenners had left their front door open, and a cat had come in during the night and was sitting on her chest looking into her eyes. She hated cats before and after that.

On the graveyard shift I would always get terribly sleepy about 4 o'clock in the morning, and then when I got off work at around 7 o'clock and the sun came up, I would be wide awake and find it very difficult to go to sleep. Even after 3 months on that shift, it was the same. I didn't see Lillian in the morning because she was going to work about the time I was coming home. Occasionally we would wave to each other as our buses passed. In the evening when she came home from work, she would wake me up to have dinner. I never quite adjusted to having dinner when I first woke up. It made me crabby, but she put up with it very well.

That was one of the coldest winters they ever had in Schenectady. Not that the temperature was so low, but it was windy all the time, and we spent a lot of awful time waiting for buses. Our principal recreation was going home to Momma on the train. Every time we saved up a little money, we spent it for train fare. It was only four hours each way.

At that time Lillian was under the care of an urologist. She had a fairly constant kidney infection with occasional fever. We tried to keep it from her parents because we didn't want them to worry. I recall on one trip back to New York, when we arrived, all four of our parents commented on how bad I looked and how good she looked. Actually she had a fever at the time, and her cheeks were rosy.

Because of the war the trains ran on a very haphazard schedule. I can remember Christmas Eve when the train we were on was about 9 hours late. Actually we weren't 9 hours late because the train was already about 5 hours late when we picked it up in Schenectady. There were people on it though, who were 9 hours late. They had expected to get home for Christmas Eve, and obviously were not going to make it before midnight. Neither did we. The train was so crowded there was hardly any standing room. There was no food in the diner, and I have a vivid recollection of one chunky guy, sprawled out in the aisle on his back snoring, with his head bouncing off the bare floor every time the train bumped. But it didn't wake him up.

The kidney infection had been diagnosed as nephritis, and was considered by Ottinger (Lillian's doctor in Schenectady) to be a terminal illness. He assured us that pregnancy was out of the question. He couldn't tell for sure how much of her kidney was gone, or if it was one kidney or both, but he knew that there was an ongoing infection there, and there was no way to stop it. Afterwards when we moved to Washington we had to get a new doctor, and that proved to be our salvation. The doctor was Herman Hoffman, one of the most remarkable medicos I have ever encountered. I'll tell you more about him later. He worked on the theory that perhaps the infection was not in the kidneys, but elsewhere, and that the kidneys were merely passing on the products of the infection. After about $3000 of medical bills (most of which did not go to him, but to people he sent Lillian to) and a year, we found it. It was something called a retrograde appendix. Nothing more than chronic appendicitis except that the appendix was in the wrong place, which made it almost impossible to diagnose. The last step in the search for the infection was that Dr. George Nordlinger opened her up for an exploratory operation, and he found and fixed the appendix. I recall that after that Dr. Hoffman said, "Okay, now you can go home and get pregnant." She did almost immediately.

I remember one evening when I was not on the night shift, very soon after we arrived in Schenectady. I heard sobs coming from that adjoining bathroom, and went in to find Lillian washing my socks. She had the wash basin full of water, and with the very tips of her fingers she was dunking my socks in the water and dropping tears into the basin at the same time. I asked her why she was crying, and she said, "At home I never even washed my own stockings."

She always hated washing socks. That seemed to her the dirtiest of all things. Later when we came to Washington, we lived in an apartment with a washing machine in the basement. I had navy socks, however, which were dark blue, and you couldn't put them in the wash with anything else because they faded all over everything. The solution to this was that I bought 30 pairs of navy socks, and once a month we'd wash them all together.

There was no drier, so they had to be hung up. There were lines strung all over the basement for people to hang their wash on, and I vividly recall that once a month there would be a forest of navy blue socks all over the basement of the apartment house.

I have two recollections of Lillian's cooking in Schenectady that are rather vivid. She really knew almost nothing about cooking, but there was a small grocery store in the neighborhood run by a German named Schultz, and when he sold her food, he would organize it into a meal and tell her how to cook it. One of these recollections involves an evening when we had company for dinner; a bachelor named Ruibal from Cuba who worked with me. Lillian made a stuffed chicken that night, and the chicken wasn't bad, but the stuffing was still cold. I've never understood how she could cook a chicken without at least warming the stuffing inside of it. The situation was greatly aggravated by the fact that Ruibal considered himself something of a cook, and delivered a long and tedious lecture on how to cook a chicken.

Ruibal also taught me, on other occasions, a reasonable assortment of Spanish curses and imprecations. I learned, for example, that in Cuba most curses are on your mother. So the Spanish word for mother, Madre, has become a curse all by itself. Therefore the word is never used in polite conversation to refer to a mother. Instead you use the word "vieja". Vieja literally translated means old female.

The other memorable cooking occasion was when Lillian decided to cook an apple pie. She had apparently got all sorts of good instructions from Schultz, and she knew that the most important part was the crust. I was there when she baked the pie, and as she bustled

around, showing off for her newlywed husband, she explained to me how important the crust was in the quality of the pie. As she put it, "The crust is 90% of the pie." Those were her very words, used over and over for emphasis, and she was surely right. When it came out of the oven, the crust was 90% of the pie. It was more like an apple butter sandwich.

Restaurants were in very short supply in Schenectady, and sometimes when we had a little extra money, but not enough for a trip to New York, we would go to Nickilaus's. That was a combination restaurant/delicatessen store that for some reason served good lobster. Lillian loved lobster. I recall the first time she ordered lobster there, she ate it in the proper manner, sucking the meat out of the lobster's legs, and emptying the claws, and really cleaning it out completely. Apparently this was very unusual in Schenectady, and Nickilaus himself came over to compliment her on the fact that she really knew how to eat a lobster.

During our time in Schenectady we played bridge almost every week with Bobby and Janet Hart. He was from Baton Rouge, La., and he told me that in Baton Rouge one could often find the following graffiti on public washroom walls. "Please flush the toilets. New Orleans needs the water." I recall Bobby Hart the first time it snowed in Schenectady. He had never seen snow in his life, and he found it the most incredible, exhilarating phenomenon. He dashed outdoors to catch it in his mouth and taste it, and catch it on his eyelashes. He really couldn't believe that there was so much of it.

Lillian was a pretty good bridge player, and enjoyed the game provided the other players were not too deadly serious. She didn't like too much complaining about her occasional errors in playing or bidding. The Harts were a very good couple at the bridge table because they didn't take it too seriously. Bourbon and soda usually went with the bridge game, and we'd have two or three apiece during the course of the bridge game. Bobby Hart once explained to me his secret formula for making a bottle of bourbon last a long time. Use a lot of ice in the drinks. They were a real nice, handsome couple, easygoing and very pleasant and sociable. Janet had the sexiest legs. Many years later when I was at White Oak (NOL), Bobby Hart stuck his head into my office to say hello. I guess I hadn't seen him in about 15 years. I didn't recognize him at first. He and Janet had broken up. I haven't seen him since, but we had a reasonable talk and lunch that day. He was back in Baton Rouge, still doing engineering with some company, I've forgotten which. He had happened to see my name someplace in connection with NOL, and had made up his mind to stop in and say hello.

Lillian loved to read; although most of the things she read were mystery stories and other things that I would consider trash. Most evenings after dinner she would let the dishes sit while she read a book until it was almost time to go to bed. Then she would turn her attention to the dishes. My feeling when we were first married was that dishes were a woman's business, but she persuaded me to help her for the sake of the "company." That is, it was very lonesome doing dishes by yourself, and if I would come in and dry them while she washed them, then we could talk and it would be much more pleasant. Somehow that got me into drying the dishes. The next thing I knew, I was washing and she was drying, and then it seems to me that most of the time I was washing and drying while she read a book. I never knew how she managed that. It was a frequent source of friction between us.

She was definitely the type that would take charge during an emergency. I'm afraid I'm not really very much good in an emergency because I'm so easy going that the fact that something really unusual, and perhaps dangerous, is going on really doesn't occur to me until it's all over. One specific example occurred after we'd come back to Washington, and were here for many years, and Floyd Brenner was born. He was born to Shirley and Lenny Brenner who shared that apartment with us in Schenectady. Floyd was having difficulty breathing, and the people in the hospital when we came to visit, didn't quite seem to know what to do about it; nor did Lenny or Shirley. Everybody was sort of wringing their hands. Lillian jumped on the phone and had our pediatrician down there in about twenty minutes. She ordered the hospital personnel to gallop off in all sorts of different directions and do all sorts of things, and they did. She must have done the right things because Floyd Brenner now has two children of his own, and he seems to be perfectly healthy and normal. Maybe he was going to make it in any case, but nobody thought so then.

A little vignette on my own capability to recognize an emergency. About a year after we came to Washington and lived on South Capitol Street, one of the neighbors woke us by banging on the door in the middle of the night. Someone driving on South Capitol Street had fallen asleep at the wheel and bashed up three cars, one of which was mine. I got in my bathrobe and slippers and walked out and looked at all the cars smashed together. I inspected them. I talked to people; and on my way back to my apartment I suddenly stopped, turned and said aloud, "My God, that was my car."

A lot of feuding and quarreling went on in the Buckner family. During all the time I knew him, Martin Buckner never talked to any of his brothers. Anna Buckner had one sister, Eva, with whom she got along reasonably well, but she and her daughter Rosalind had a quarrel that went on and off. As the years went by, it got more on than off, and I think for the last 5 or 6 years they didn't talk to each other, hardly at all. Lillian was always the peacemaker between them, and when we'd come to New York, one of our chores was always to try to patch up the current problem between Rosalind and Nanny.

I can scarcely remember the subjects of any of these quarrels, except the last one, but that is perhaps illustrative. Someone said at one time or another that Rosalind and her mother looked like sisters. Rosalind resented this. Nanny's reaction was, "Why should she not want me to be her sister? Ain't I a good-looking woman?"

Lillian was always a woman's woman in the sense that any time there was a quarrel between a man and a woman; she took the woman's side. She used to play mah-jongg with the "girls" one night a week, and they would exchange incredible confidences, having to do with their love lives and everything else. Sometimes I would get, what seemed to me, smatterings of these confidences; and although they were only smatterings, I knew an awful lot of embarrassing things about the women she played mah-jongg with; all the way down to their orgasms or lack of them.

These mah-jongg games went on until the small hours of the morning on week nights. When the game was in our house, it was my custom to go to sleep, and sometimes complain the next day about how noisy they were. When we lived on Aragon Lane, they would play in the den, or the aggravation room as I sometimes called it, and my bedroom was at the very other end of the house. So they disturbed me very little. You can get some idea of how little they disturbed me from the following event. One night they emptied an ashtray into the little plastic trash basket in the kitchen. A cigarette was still smoldering in the ashtray, and the basket caught fire. Part of the house was filled with smoke. The door jam in the kitchen burned up, and the fire insurance expenses were about $2000. I found out about it in the morning.

The kitchen sink had one of those sprayers on it for spraying dishes. The fire was very near the sink. Fortunately somebody thought of turning that sprayer on the fire, and they put it out without having to call the fire department. That would have wakened me - I think.

We went to Las Vegas at least twice, but the first time was the most exciting. We were traveling across the country with Melvin and Brian. The girls were not yet born. We had been camping, and mostly going to bed by 9 or 10 o'clock at night. We checked into this elegant hotel. I think it was The Sahara or The Sands, with a huge gambling casino. I noticed the menu for The Hunt Breakfast, which was served between midnight and 4 A.M., and I was hoping we could stay up until midnight so I could enjoy that breakfast. We put the kids to bed in the hotel room. They were old enough then that we didn't need a babysitter, and we went down to the casino. It turned out that staying up until midnight was no problem. The real problem was dragging Lillian away from the 21 table before 4 A.M. when they closed The Hunt Breakfast. I just made it. By then she had won enough money at the 21 table to pay for all my losses at craps and everything else, and also pay for the weekend. She was terribly exhilarated, and never could go to sleep at all that night. About 8 A.M. she took Melvin and Brian to the swimming pool and stayed with them while I got a few more hours sleep.

Our second trip to Las Vegas was many years later. Lillian's enjoyment was spoiled by two things, one of which was that she didn't win, and the other was an oriental fellow, who had something to do with Hawaiian sugar, they told us. This fellow watched her play for a few minutes and then asked if he could bet with her. She said no. Then he went to the croupier and had him explain to Lillian what he meant by betting with her. He had no intention of influencing her decisions about whether to draw or split, or anything of that type: he just wanted his money to ride with whatever she did. The croupier urged her to do that, and she did. She was betting a dollar or two on a card, and he dropped a hundred dollar bill in front of her to ride with her dollar. That really spoiled it. In some subtle way, it took all the pleasure out of her playing, and she didn't remain at the table very long.

I recall a related experience many years later when we were in Scotland, and we went to dinner and dancing as we often did, on the recommendation of a guy who owned the little hotel we were staying in. He assured us that the only place that had a good meal and dancing was one that also had a gambling casino. We had a nice dinner and danced, and before we left, we went to the casino. When we arrived there was only one person playing at the roulette tables. He was betting about 100 pounds on each roll. Of course this stopped everyone else. Everyone was watching him. I went over to the cash chip window to ask the guy who that was, and he told me that he was a local fellow who bought up and straightened out failing businesses. When I asked him the man's name I thought he said Cullen, but I asked him to spell it, and he spelled C-O-H-E-N.

I taught Lillian to drive. It was sometime after we arrived in Washington and were living in Anacostia. I had bought a 1940 Plymouth. She was always a hard driver, although apparently good because she never had any serious accidents. When she was learning, though, I remember driving with her along the road that borders The Anacostia River, on the Anacostia side. It was a nice road, but it suddenly turned right to go over The South Capitol Street Bridge. The turn was very sharp, so I said to her, "Slow down — slow down — slow down." She hit that curve at about 35 mph. Fortunately there was parkland on the far side of the curve with no ditches or anything, because she never could make the curve, and off we went across the fields.

Whenever I was away on a business trip, I knew that Lillian didn't really expect fidelity of me. She always considered that an affair of that type was no threat to her marriage. On the other hand, it was clearly my responsibility to make sure that she never found out about it if such an affair occurred. I recall one time that there was an envelope in my luggage (she always packed for me when I went on a trip), and on the envelope was written, "Just in case," and inside was a condom. Of course, a condom was still in my luggage when I came back.

In 1957 Lillian and I made our first trip to Europe. I had some business in Naples with the bathyscaphe, and I was going to be there about a week. Then she would meet me and we would vacation in Italy, France, Switzerland and England. All of that happened, except that the arrangements were rather haphazard. We had trouble arranging the portion of her flight from Rome to Naples, so we arranged for her to come by train, and I would meet the train. Because we knew of no hotels there, our emergency arrangements were that in case we couldn't contact each other for some reason, we would both get in touch with the U.S. Naval Attaché in Naples. Now, as it turns out, there isn't any U.S. Naval Attaché in Naples.

After I arrived in Naples I discovered that we simply didn't have the right flight schedule, and that there was indeed a connecting flight from Rome to Naples. So I sent her a telegram telling her about it, and in addition, arranged for a message to be left for her at the Rome airport telling her to take the plane. I had figured the schedule out pretty carefully, and I could meet the plane, and in case she didn't get one of those messages, I still had time to meet the train.

Not having any luggage, and having been told that you could get to the Naples airport by streetcar, I tried out my Italian in an effort to do that. I had lots of time. I remember the scene on the streetcar. There were lots of people crowding, and I was one of the last people to get on. Behind me was a little kid who I thought was stuck in the door. Actually the kid did not want to get on. He didn't want to pay the fare; so half in and half out was where he wanted to be. Then if the conductor came to grab him, he could get off and run. I didn't understand that, so I tried to open the door. I pulled on it as hard as I could, and it sort of buckled. I broke the glass. It was a sort of Toonerville Trolley type of streetcar anyhow, and when the glass came tumbling down, everybody starting talking to each other in Italian in loud voices. I found one quiet fellow next to me, and I said to him in Italian, "What should I do?"

He looked at me like I was crazy and said, "Nothing." I got off at the next stop through the same door without getting close to the driver or paying a fare. I took a cab to the airport.

The cab driver asked me if I wanted him to wait. I thought that was a stupid question to have a cab wait at an airport. But when I saw the airport, I realized that was not such a bad idea, and I asked him to wait. The Naples airport was hardly more than a dirt strip. The plane was thoroughly late, and when I ascertained that Lillian was, in fact, not on it, I made a dash for the cab, and we headed for the railroad station. The railroad station was a huge, complicated, impressive building, and the cab driver, who by this time was my bosom buddy although I had not paid him anything, was obviously going to wait again. He was not worried that I was going to cheat him out of his money. What he was worried about was that I wouldn't find him in this huge station. I remember him pointing out to me that he would be waiting under one particular big sign. He also told me what track the train was coming in on and how to get there.

I got to the track as the passengers were getting off, and checked them all. But Lillian was not there. Now the situation was getting desperate. I ascertained that there was some slight possibility that her plane might have come into Rome early so that she could have got on an earlier train, the "Rapido." I went to the 1st class waiting room, and she was not there either. I wandered around the railroad station asking people what to do. I looked in the phone book for the Naval Attaché's office, and that's when I discovered there wasn't any, and as a last desperate move I tried the 2nd and 3rd class waiting rooms. And there she was, in the 3rd class waiting room. She had indeed gotten into Rome early, made a mad dash across Rome in a taxi-cab, and had gotten on the Rapido, which goes non-stop from Rome to Naples. She had been in that waiting room about two hours. She also knew by then that there was no Naval Attaché in Naples. She was sitting in this 3rd class waiting room, which she thought was the only one, surrounded by people with bundles eating lunches and smelling of garlic. She had a soft cover book that she was reading with some sort of a lurid picture on the cover, and when I came in, she looked up from the book, saw me, and returned her gaze to the book.

I sat down beside her, and I think it was a full day before I convinced her of what had really happened, and that I hadn't missed meeting her because I was involved with some other woman. The cab driver was so glad to see her he almost kissed her. That's one of the things I loved about Neopolitans; cheating an American was to them like cheating the phone company, but when a man can't find his wife — that they really sympathize with.

We stayed one night in Naples and then went to Capri. I think it's a terrible mistake to start a tour of Europe from a place like Capri, particularly if you have no specific reservations and arrangements. The place hypnotizes you. I don't recall how many days we stayed there, but I do recall the waiter at the Piazza Umberto saying to us as we came down for our late afternoon Compari and soda on at least two occasions, "Don't tell me, I know — tomorrow you're leaving."

Our routine was to have breakfast in our room and leave there at about 11 in the morning. Then we would walk to the Marina Piccola, where we would have a swim and lunch at about 2 o'clock. Then we would take the bus back to our hotel, change, and get ready for the main business of the day, which was sitting in the Piazza, drinking Compari sodas, and deciding where we were going to have dinner. It was delightfully monotonous. The sun came up every morning, went through the sky, and went down at night. It was in September, 1957. I remember the date because that's when Sputnik went up, and everybody wanted to talk to me because I was an American. They wanted to know how we Americans could let the Russians get ahead of us like that. All the Europeans I talked to seemed to have the distinct feeling that we had let them down.

For several months before the trip I made an effort to learn Italian by studying from tourist records. What I managed to do was to get the accent really good, but I had almost no comprehension of what was said to me. I recall when we were in Venice asking some woman where the railroad station was, and the answer went by me like a shot. As I reconstructed it later, it seemed to me that what she said was something like, "The railroad station — I haven't been there for a long time. The last time I was near there was at my sister's wedding. She married a guy that was no good —." That's a far cry from, "Go down two blocks and turn left." Maybe that was at the end of the speech, but I had lost the bubble before she got to it.

Actually, Lillian was much better at understanding Italian than I was, even though she knew nothing about the language. Somehow from the facial expressions and the general context, she would know what was being talked about; like whether it was a joke or something serious. She would piece together little gestures and things. Many times she explained to me what was said in Italian even though she didn't know a word of it.

Lillian rarely made me breakfast, but she would get out of bed and come talk to me while I was eating it. I made a rule at one time. If she made me breakfast we would talk while I ate. Otherwise I would read the paper. Sometimes I actually made the rule stick.

We always wanted to have four children. I guess that was because my mother had had four children and her mother had had four children. About two years after Brian was born, she miscarried a child. That didn't upset us too much, but about two years after that she miscarried again, and we began to think there was something wrong. In fact there was nothing wrong, as the doctor explained afterwards. A certain fraction of conceptions miscarry, and there's some chance that a perfectly healthy couple can have two in a row. I remember that for some reason Herman Hoffman wanted to check my sperm at that point. I brought it to him in a condom. It was very embarrassing. The little things seemed to be swimming around okay I guess. I don't know what other tests he was equipped to make in those days.

Lillian was always very meticulous about her appearance. She kept her weight very carefully within limits and got a reasonable amount of exercise, although she smoked very heavily all her life. I remember when she decided to dye her hair blond; I pretended not to notice it, although she had discussed it with me before. I thought it was lovely, really, once I got used to it. You can tell about when that was by the home movies we have. I particularly recall Brian looking at the pictures taken before Lillian dyed her hair and asking who that woman was.

I remember the night she found the lump on her breast and showed it to me. It was quite visible; a roughness, an irregularity that affected the skin surface, and when you touched it, you could feel it was hard. She went to the doctor the very next morning, and the operation was performed either that day or the next. We were told that the prognosis was good, but in fact, as we found out about a year later, it was already too late.

The night that I brought her back from the hospital with bandages where her left breast had been, she was feeling less than a woman, and quite depressed. That was the only time in my life I actually prayed for an erection; and we did have very satisfactory sex that night. I felt that it was the most important thing in my life to show her, at that time, how things were going to be between us.

In fact our life did go on pretty much the same after the operation. We went on a wonderful tour to Hawaii with the

United Airlines stockholders, where we danced a lot and drank a lot of Mai Tais. In fact, every time something went wrong with the arrangements, like the weather was too rough for a catamaran ride we were supposed to take, they would give us a cocktail party instead. I think at the end they owed us three cocktail parties which they put back to back. That was a disaster for some of the tour members. We got in with a nice group of four couples; who I really don't remember any more, but we did have a fine time.

One scientific curiosity I remember from that trip was that at one point there was a huge storm someplace out in the Pacific, and large waves were generated which traveled about a thousand miles before they reached the Hawaiian shore. They were large enough to do considerable damage to the buildings along the coast. In fact they broke the windows of the dining room of the hotel we were staying in, and water was all over the dining room floor so we had to eat someplace else. The amazing thing about it was that that was the only part of the storm we ever saw. While the waves were beating up the beach and all the houses along it, the weather was clear and sunny, and there was almost no wind.

Another strange thing about the Hawaiian vacation was that when we got back, we arrived at Baltimore Airport and took the limousine into Silver Spring where Brian met us with the station wagon. Someplace before getting into the limousine I met a neighbor of mine, and we offered him a ride from Silver Spring home. He accepted. When we got to Silver Spring, I put his luggage in the station wagon with ours. I was a little irritated that he made no effort to lift his own suitcase. When we got to his house, he got out of the car and waved, and started into his house. I called after him, "You forgot your luggage."

He said, "I don't have any luggage."

We had picked up somebody else's luggage at the limousine stop, and when we got home I had to take it back, or I guess Brian took it back.

We also had a very lovely vacation in England, where we stopped at Hurley Manor, which was a very old but simple country hotel with fields around it and a stable. I suggested we do a little horseback riding while we were there, and Lillian declined. At that point I had some inkling that her back was bothering her. By the time of our 25th wedding anniversary party, which was a marvelous affair, with all our friends and relatives coming from all over, it was quite clear to me that her back was bothering her. She may have known long before that, when we were in England, but after the 25th wedding anniversary party, I knew too.

During her last few months, she assured me over and over with great sincerity that I had been a wonderful husband, and she left me with no guilt. The only thing she wanted was that I set up some kind of a trust for the girls' education in case I married again. She wanted them to be taken care of. She was not worried about the boys because they already had their education, or at least their opportunity.

During her final stay at the hospital, she had me take her in the wheelchair to the hospital library where she asked the librarian if there was a book on how to tell children about terminal illness. At the end she was a pitiful sight in that hospital bed. They had given her chemo-therapy, and she had lost her hair. But, of course, we had a wig made which she wore for at least several weeks. The wig was askew on her head. The tumor in her stomach had grown to the point where the diaphragm no longer worked properly, and she was struggling for every breath. She could not talk properly, either because of the growths in her mouth, or because of the narcotics they had given her. I sat at her bedside for a while, but I couldn't tolerate the indignity that was being heaped upon her. The nurse came in, and I told her very authoritatively to pull the tubes out and let the poor woman die. The tubes were taken out of her veins, and I don't think she lived twenty minutes after that. For some strange reason I recall walking around the hospital buildings along the grass, close to the brick of the buildings before I came back in.

# JULIE RUBIN

Julie Rubin is, without doubt, my longest time friend. My mother and his mother met through a mutual friend named Fannie Lassman when we lived at 1545 Jesup Avenue and he lived a half a dozen houses away on Jesup Avenue. We used to play ball together in the street. Neither of us were very athletic. We would always call for each other after school. Julie was a grade ahead of me. We had a bird whistle we used to give to call each other. To kids it sounded like a bird. We worked up wild schemes like building telephones between the houses, and we actually did build two boats together when we were in high school; sailboats. One of them really sailed, but it was terribly tipsy; the other one wasn't tipsy, but it didn't sail. At any rate we had great adventures in Spuytendyvel Creek where The Harlem River joins The Hudson at the top of Manhattan, not very far from George Washington High School. We used to keep the boat nearby in Sherman Creek, which is still there, and there is a power station there. I don't know if they keep boats there or not, but you can see it as you go by on The Major Deegan Expressway. You can see George Washington High School on the hill, and below it Sherman Creek.

I remember that I had the distinction of fainting at Julie Rubin's Bar Mitzvah. I had a seat on the aisle, and there were long periods of standing when the Ark was opened or when The Shmonah Esrai was being said. During one of these periods of standing I simply fell like a log into the aisle. In my younger days I had Hypoglycemia, although I don't think anyone diagnosed it correctly. It wasn't a very serious ailment, but it would hit me once in a while with a fainting spell. Julie still remembers the occasion. I really stopped the ceremony.

Julie majored in accounting, and when he got out of school he went to work for his father, who made corsets. Those were something like girdles, but they had stays in them, originally made of whale bone, later of steel. They are now completely out of style, and they were going out of style during that period. Working for his father, Julie noticed that there was a certain machine (which I think they called a "finishing machine") which was something like a vacuum cleaner and an electric razor put together. When the workers finished with a garment there were still lots of loose threads attached. They would pass the garment over this thing, and it would suck the loose threads up and cut them off, resulting in a finished garment. These machines were terribly expensive, and they came with a table and a stand and very fancy arms. Julie thought he could make one a helluva lot simpler and cheaper. In fact he put one together out of a vacuum cleaner and an electric razor and it worked very well.

The problem was that the company that made them had all sorts of patents, but Julie decided to chance it and try to sell them anyhow because his price was so much lower. His attitude was, "One day they'll catch up with me, but in the meanwhile I can make a living out of it." That was right after World War II. He's been making a living at it ever since, and a very good living, and he's still waiting for them to catch up to him with their patents, which have by now expired.

Julie was a B-26 bomber pilot in WW II, flying missions over Germany, mainly from Italy. He flew 75 missions at a time when only 50 were required. His argument was a typically modest one, "The war here is going to end before the war in The Pacific, and those pilots that have flown 50 missions will be the first ones to have to go and fly in The Pacific. When I finish here, I don't ever want to fly again." Besides he said, "At this stage of the war I'm flying mostly milk runs. Who knows what's going on in Japan?" I recall the letter in which he humorously protested that, "They're shooting at me. Me! Your friend Julie. They're trying to kill me."

After the war he married Phyllis, partly on my recommendation. I recall we were up at my father's place in Lake Mohegan with about 5 couples one Sunday, and having a lot of fun. Phyllis was there. Someone had brought her, possibly as a date for Julie. We played "Charades," and at one point Phyllis was doing waves on the water with her arms and knees waving gracefully. I thought she was absolutely the most charming thing I had seen in a long time. I recall saying to Julie, "You better marry that girl." I could speak with some authority at that time because I was already married to Lillian.

Julie and Phyllis were married for quite a number of years without children, and they finally adopted Ellen. That was a bit of a hassle because according to law her mother (Ellen's mother) had a year in which to change her mind. The adoption was one of these not quite legal things as I recall. Her mother may have gone into the hospital and registered as Mrs. Rubin. I'm not quite sure about that. In any case, shortly after they adopted Ellen, they had two children of their own. Something rather similar happened to Myron Joseph, because he adopted his first daughter after they had no children for a long time, and then they had one of their own. Julie's genetic daughters are Carol and Laura. Carol was married to Steve, and before they were married, they lived together for a long time. They were both teaching school, and they lived together here in Washington. I really didn't want to have very much to do with them because they were living together unmarried. In those days I was very straight laced about that kind of thing. After they got married, I invited them over and tried to be more friendly with them, but by then they had their own circle of friends, and my friendship wasn't very important. Their marriage didn't last. Julie took Steve (Carol's husband) into his business at one point, and I understand they didn't get along very well. I don't think that had anything to do with the breakup of the marriage. They are all very beautiful and devoted girls.

Sometime after Lillian died and I went to visit Julie and Phyllis for a few days. I was reminiscing a bit about one thing and another. One of the things which came to mind was that as a child I always thought roller skating was the greatest thing in the world, and I didn't understand why adults didn't roller-skate. To me, at that age, there was nothing more exhilarating than roller-skating. I was telling this to Julie and Phyllis to illustrate how different a child's point of view and an adult's are. Laura was listening to the conversation, and she went into her room and hauled out two pair of roller skates; one for me and one for her. By God I got them on and roller-skated around the block a couple of times with her.

That reminded me of the quotation from Lowell Green, which you will find someplace in this document, "Your muscles never forget."

This past summer I went to Laura's wedding in Julie's backyard. I took Barbara, and it was very nice to see the gang all together. We had a real fine time.

Julie's father Sam, as a youth, was the tough on the block. He served in the peacetime army and was a little uncouth. Julie's mother was a schoolteacher who worshipped culture. She never would have married Sam except that she couldn't seem to keep any other suitors interested. One date is all she got from any of them. In later years she found out that Sam would be waiting nearby whenever a date took her home. When the guy left he would warn him to, "Stay away from my girl," and maybe even rough him up a bit.

# THE TIME I SLEPT WITH
# SIMONE COUSTEAU

In the late 50s and early 60s I was head of The Systems Analysis Group of The Undersea Warfare R&D Planning Council. The Council was, in fact, a council of laboratories involved in undersea warfare, including government and non-government labs like Woods Hole, Hudson Labs of Columbia U, and The Applied Physics Lab of The University of Washington. I had a staff of 3 officers, 6 civilians and three secretaries, and was housed at The Naval Ordnance laboratory, which was one of the government labs included in the council. The council had four meetings per year, always in interesting places and, of course, I always went and frequently brought some of my people. Further, since my Systems Analysis Group was the only staff of The Council, I had some responsibility for the arrangements for the meetings and the technical content. I got to know some pretty important people in that job. Bob Frosch, Alan Berman, Paul Frye and Greg Hartmann were at one time or another chairmen of the council and my boss. That was, I always said, the best job in The U.S. Navy, and I only left to start Raff Associates.

This story is about one meeting the Council had at the NATO Laboratory in La Spezia, Italy, to which Jacques Cousteau was invited and came. It was not uncommon for council members to bring their wives (at their own expense), and Jacques brought Simone.

The first day of the meetings went very badly. Several of the lab directors came into conflict with each other and things were unhappy all around. That night was the planned social event. We had one at every meeting. This was a boat trip to a restaurant at Porto Venerie across the bay. I thought that some alcohol on the boat would raise everyone's spirits, so I bought a lot of beer and took it aboard, only to discover that there were no glasses on the boat and the beer was in quart bottles. I carefully considered what to do to get all these important people to swig from bottles and decided that I merely needed someone to start. Simone Cousteau was the best bet, and I took the top off the first bottle and passed it to her. She took a swig and passed it on and the problem was solved.

Things got better after that. The boat trip was fine; so was the meal and the rest of the meeting. At the end Jacques invited us to visit his lab at Monaco. At that time he was starting a hydrofoil ferry service along the Cote D'Azure and he offered to take us from La Spezia to Monaco in a hydrofoil. About six of us accepted the offer.

The boat had a large open passengers' compartment with upholstered benches at the center and around the sides which I settled into after I had had a tour of the bridge and machinery and an explanation of how it all worked. It was a sunny afternoon and the scenery was monotonous, so I dozed off. It seemed only a short while before we were at the harbor in Monaco.

Jacques took us on a tour of his laboratory. It was beautiful. All the lab rooms were carved into a cliff overlooking The Mediterranean. He told us what was going on in each room (about a dozen) and what was important about it, what they hoped to find out, and he answered our questions. He was very impressive.

Of course we had to change our return tickets from La Spezia to Monaco, and Simone took care of that by phone, but when we got to the airport they laughed at us. How could we have made reservations that morning, at the height of the season, when all the flights had been booked for months? I said, "We were told we had reservations on this flight."

The ticket agent snickered, "Who told you that you had reservations?"

"Simone Cousteau."

That did it. A look of awe came over the ticket agent's face and they put us all on the flight.

Oh! About the title — at one time while I was dozing in the cockpit of the hydrofoil I noticed Simone asleep about ten feet away on the same bench.

# THE SINAI AND EGYPT

After Anna and I split up, Terri was at The Hebrew University in Jerusalem where she was very unhappy and wanted to come home. She also wanted me to come and visit her there. She intended to come back with me. She tried all sorts of travel arrangements to lure me there, and the thing that finally won was a one week camel trip in The Sinai Desert. It was being arranged by The Hebrew University for students and parents. I went and enjoyed it enormously. There were about 120 students, and one parent, me. One of the reasons I wanted to go was because I wanted the feel of the desert for the novel I was writing.

It was a pretty rough trip in the sense of being uncivilized. We didn't have tents, but slept in sleeping bags on the ground, and it was quite cold. We have a lot of pictures we took. I would guess that in the 5 days that we were actually in The Sinai itself, we walked well over 100 miles. The camels mostly carried water and baggage. There were supposed to be more camels, but it was the last trip before they gave The Sinai back to Egypt, and the Bedouin who supplied the camels weren't terribly cooperative because they knew there was no future in it for them.

It has always seemed to me that Middle-Easterners, be they Israelis or Arabs, and be they at home or in Bank Leumi in New York, have a somewhat different attitude towards inquiries and problems than Americans. Their objective is to get rid of you. The Americans have an objective to help. A case in point was after we came back from the camel trip, we were supposed to go to Egypt for a few days; but the camel trip ended at the beginning of the Sabbath. We didn't have our tickets, and we didn't have a visa for Terri. I had gotten a visa in Washington, but she neglected to get hers.

We were flying on Nefrititi Airlines, which it turns out, has no offices at the airports either in Cairo or Tel Aviv. They fly every other day. We tried to call them from our hotel in Jerusalem and couldn't find the number. I went down to the hotel desk to look in the phone book with Terri, who is pretty good at Hebrew, and discovered to my chagrin that the phone book we were looking at was 5 years old. That was the newest phone book they had in that big hotel.

We tried calling half a dozen places, like El Al and the embassies, but all we got was people who wanted you to go away. We went around the loop. Somebody would give us a phone number. We would call that one. They would give us another phone number. We would call that and they would suggest the phone number we called originally.

Finally I had the idea of calling TWA because I had flown over on that airline, and I thought that gave me a little bit of a claim on them. I called and I got a guy with a bit of a Brooklyn accent, and I knew I was home. He listened to the problem. He sympathized. He, first of all, assured us that you didn't need a visa to go to Egypt unless you aren't going to change any money at the airport. All they're interested in is money, so if you change about a hundred dollars into Egyptian pounds at the official exchange rate when you arrive in Cairo, you don't need a visa. The tickets were a little bit more of a problem, but he had a good idea about that too. He said, "You know there are not only Israeli ticket agents, but there are Arab ticket agents." He located one for us. We went there in Jerusalem, and sure enough they were open on Friday afternoon and we got our tickets. Later, when we missed our flight coining back from Egypt and had to rearrange things, we had a very similar experience. Nobody was of any help until we met an American at the Cairo Airport who had something to do with Nefrititi Airlines. He straightened everything out and we boarded the plane the next day.

There was one other illustrative experience which I backed into just for the sake of being mean. The last hotel we stayed at in Cairo was the Concorde near the airport, and the hotel bill was about $100. I really wanted to put that on my credit card because

I was short of money. I assured the cashier that The Rameses Hilton, where we had stayed for 3 days in Cairo, had taken my credit card, and suggested he call them. He told me he couldn't take my credit card but he would call. He called and checked and finally said that he would not take the credit card. I then said that I didn't have any cash, which I thought would leave him with no alternative. Well, he didn't have any alternative, but he wouldn't let us leave the hotel. They took our bags and put them behind the counter. So we waited. At this point it was more of an adventure to me than anything else, and I was trying to find out what would happen. Presently it came time for our airplane to leave, and we really had to go catch it, so I produced $100 in cash after I had told him I didn't have any.

His reaction was very interesting. I rather think an American would have been angry at my having lied, but the cashier was merely grateful. The fact that I had lied didn't seem to bother him at all, or enter into his calculations. He personally carried our luggage out to the cab and expressed his gratitude over and over.

# TOM JOHNSON

Tom Johnson was my Aunt Jeanette's second husband. He was an old line southern gentleman, and spoke that way, and was the absolute soul of courtesy. He was a little round fat man who smoked cigarettes in a cigarette holder with the ashes falling on his vest. I have very fond memories of him because he was Hospitality Manager at The Taft Hotel in New York at a time when I was of dating age and always looking for places to take girls. Tom had an endless supply of tickets to radio broadcasts. With the ticket you could become part of the studio audience, and it was as good as a show but free. I took a lot of dates to shows with Uncle Tom's tickets.

I recall that when I would drop in to pick up tickets, he would always make me feel as though I had done him the greatest favor in the world. Whatever was going on in his office at the time the secretary announced my presence would be interrupted while he came out to shake my hand and tell me how glad he was that I had come to see him, "And would I like some tickets to a broadcast, by the way?"

Of course I always did. And he knew very well that that was why I came there, but I never had to bring up the subject, and he always acted like I was doing him a favor. He was the soul of a hotel hospitality manager. He and Aunt Jeanette were happily married until he died.

# THE GOVERNMENT CHECK
# THAT WENT ASTRAY

Early in the history of The Bethesda Corporation we did a study for NSWC and had some trouble getting our payment. One day we received a call from someone at The Bethesda Armature Company. He had the check. It was sent to him by mistake made out to The Bethesda Corporation. As usual with such government checks, it came alone in an envelope with no explanation of what it was for and the only address on it was The Bethesda Armature Company; but he tracked us down.

We needed the money and I was very grateful. I offered to take him to lunch, but he declined. I then insisted on visiting to thank him personally. He was an elderly man with suspenders. We had a cup of coffee together in his office. At one point in the conversation I said, "How on earth could they have made such a mistake?"

His reply was exactly as follows:  "Now, I'm not a bigot, but I'll tell you; when they took the shovels away from those niggers, they ruined them."

# THE BASE ANGLES

Melvin spoke very early in life, and he was a normal sized kid. His speech was always very impressive to people. As a sort of a lark I taught him, very shortly after he learned to say "Mommy" and "Daddy", to say, "The base angles of an isosceles triangle are equal." The cue for this was, "Melvin, tell them about geometry." He would come forth with this statement with great aplomb. The problem was that people didn't expect a kid to say something like that, so they had difficulty understanding him even though he said it well.

When Brian was about the same age I tried something a little more adventurous. The cue was, "Tell them about Caesar." He would come forth with the statement, "Omnia gaula divisa est en partes tres." That is the opening line of something in Latin about Caesar. That turned out to be even worse of a disaster for the same reason, and also because most people didn't recognize the line even if they heard it distinctly.

# MRS. GOLDSMITH

Mrs. Goldsmith is Eli's mother, she is now in her nineties, but she is still a very quiet, pleasant and charming woman, although her body doesn't work very well anymore. The story I like best about her has to do with Lynn, Sylvia's second daughter, who was never quite right. She was not really retarded, but she had some of the symptoms. For Eli and Sylvia and Mrs. Goldsmith, she was the main problem issue of their lives. They always prayed that she would marry some nice guy who would take care of her.

After Harry Goldsmith died, Mrs. Goldsmith made a trip to Israel. It was her first trip, and when she came back, Eli, who was always an extremely devoted child, met her at the airport. He had great news for her; Lynn was engaged. He met her, and that was almost the first thing he said, "Mama, Lynn is engaged."

She said, "I know."

He said, "How could you know? You've been gone all this time."

She said, "I put a note in the wall."

# VISION

When I reached the age when I needed reading glasses I fought it for a long time before I gave in. One day I was shaving and I happened to be wearing the glasses. I was startled. I had forgotten that you could see the individual hairs in your beard.

# THE CENTER OF THE EARTH

At some time in my life (and you can guess when from the story) there was a little grocery store across the street from our house on E 179th Street in The Bronx. It was what we would call today a convenience store. In those days you didn't take things off the shelves; the storekeeper took them off the shelves. You told him what you wanted, and he took them down from his side of the counter, put them on the counter, added up the price on the bag with a pencil from behind his ear; and then you paid him and went away with the bag. The pencil went back behind his ear. I recall that things were a little more expensive there than in the bigger stores, but it was almost right across the street, and we used to go there for rolls and milk and things like that.

On the customers' side of the counter, on the floor, there was a brass circle about 4" in diameter. It was flush with the floor, and obviously covered some sort of a hole which had been left at some time by remodeling of the store. Maybe a pipe came through there at one time. I was there with my brother Eddie, and I asked him what that brass plate was for. He thought a minute and explained that it was a marker to indicate that that spot was directly above the center of the earth.

It seemed an extraordinary distinction for our little grocery store, and I really didn't believe him. When we got home I checked with Pop. He assured me that that spot in the grocery store was directly above the center of the earth. For some time I was awed by that fact.

# THAT'S FAITH!

I was told by an Italian Catholic in Rome that the church is responsible for all the troubles in Italy. "They're corrupt. They oppress the poor and they waste the contributions of the people; but what can you do? Those bastards have got the keys to The Kingdom of Heaven."

Marie Henig, a Catholic who lived in the same apartment house as the Buckners, across from Poe Park in The Bronx, had a new Catholic nephew in 1947. They decided to circumcise him for health reasons. After some thought they opted for a Moyel instead of a doctor. "The moyel does that all the time, and he's an expert."

They found one who would do it. But when they discussed the fee, they found it was no cheaper than for Jewish kids even though he didn't have to say the prayers. Being basically frugal people who hated to see anything go to waste, they wanted the prayers too. "For the same money, why not? Prayers can't hurt."

# NINA'S SWIMMING TROPHY

When Nina was about 5 years old, she and Lillian and I went to The Concord Hotel for about a week. I think Mel and Brian were at camp. The Concord Hotel is a very elegant place, but I learned that one should never spend a week there. Three days is a maximum because they tempt you with this magnificent variety of food, and after three days you're so full and tired of eating that you begin to feel sick. They had three swimming pools; one was heated for their guests who liked to swim in warm water; one was unheated for their guests who liked to swim in cold water; and one was empty. I suppose that was because some of their guests didn't swim.

The swimming instructor at The Concord was Buster Crabbe. If the name is familiar, it's because he played the lead role in some of the later Tarzan movies. In the earlier movies the role was played by Johnny Weismuller, also a champion swimmer. However Buster Crabbe only came up on weekends, and he would give a little swimming demonstration and some lessons.

At that time Nina was already a pretty fair swimmer, but she was small for her age, and people were continuously surprised at her ability to swim. The workday swimming instructor had picked Nina out for a demonstration swimming lesson, somewhat fraudulently.

When the great demonstration came, there were about 100 people around the pool, and Buster Crabbe dove in and swam about a length and a half with magnificent form, and then stopped up to his waist in shallow water and said, "Not bad for a grandfather, Aye?"

He then went on to talk about how easy it was with his method to teach children to swim, and that there was a little girl in the audience who was about ready to learn. He then turned toward Nina and said, "Alright Honey, I'm gonna teach you to swim," and as he started toward her, she dove off the side of the pool in a racing dive and swam toward him. There was a shower of laughter from the people around the side of the pool, and Buster Crabbe grabbed a trophy from somewhere and stuck it in Nina's hand.

# FRANKLIN AT 8

At that age, I drove Franklin up to Connecticut for a long weekend, and the trip was miserable. It took about 45 minutes to get on the beltway from Snug Hill Lane. It was raining. There were accidents all over. That was very irritating to both me and him, but in addition he had made a little duck that he had wanted to bring to Barbara, and he had forgotten it. He also would have liked to bring his bicycle with us, but we thought of it too late. This combination of circumstances had him really depressed, and he complained — and complained — and complained. About two hours out, by which time we had not quite reached the far side of Baltimore, he had a thought and said, "Here I am complaining, and you're the one who has to drive in all this nasty rain and traffic. It must be much worse for you than for me." After that he didn't complain for the rest of the trip.

Sometime on the weekend we went to The Apple Festival, which was in a high school called Staples. They had all sorts of amusements and games. One of them was a golf game; a fairly straightforward thing in which you got a putter, one ball for a quarter, three balls for 50c, and 7 balls for a dollar. We stood there watching a girl, quite a bit bigger than Franklin, trying desperately to get one of seven balls in the hole, and she never did succeed. Franklin seemed very interested, so I gave him 50c and said, "Why don't you get three balls?"

He said, "I only need one."

And indeed he walked up, played his quarter, got one ball and set it down. He looked at it very carefully, walked around it, took a few practice swings and dropped it right in the hole.

The onlookers were very impressed. I congratulated him on this fine and outstandingly impressive performance, but he assured me over and over again that it was just luck.

He has quite a knack of making things with string. His cutest is a little puppet show about a fire that goes on in front of a cardboard carton on the dining room table. First he tells you there's a fire, and while he is hidden by the carton a teddy bear on top of it yells, "Fire!" Then a fire truck comes out from behind a smaller box in front of the carton. Another bear comes off the fire truck and climbs up to the top of the carton and rescues the bear that was yelling.

# CHRISTMAS

In my family when I was growing up, Christmas was just another day; but Lillian's family made a thing out of it. They would all assemble for the holiday and exchange gifts. There would be great excitement including, in the early days before Lillian and I had any children, a crap game which would involve George, Seymour, Martin, Jerry and me. It usually went on and on until the small hours of the morning or until Martin's knees gave out. There was even, on many of these occasions, a fake Christmas tree. This was something Jerry had bought. It was about a foot and a half high with lights built into it, and it used to be set on the baby grand piano and plugged into a socket. The lights would twinkle in different colors.

Martin's father, Mendell, who was also Carl's grandfather and Shirley's grandfather, was a very religious man; kosher and all of that. Melvin was named after him. He was also a very forceful and straightforward guy. I remember every time I'd go to see him, among the first four or five questions he would ask me was, "How much money do you make?1 Of course I never wanted to tell him the truth, but then the next time I couldn't remember the lie I told him before, and I was sure he did remember.

There was always a fear at these Christmas parties that Grandpa would show up unexpectedly. The piano with the little tree on it was in straight sight of the entrance to the apartment door (on the Grand Concourse opposite Poe Park). So all during Christmas, anytime there was a knock on the door, the suspicion was that it might be Mendell (Grandpa). I recall that with every knock on the door would come a yell, "Just a minute!" and we would all hold our breath while Jerry made a dash for that Christmas tree, unplugged it, and stuck it in the closet. Then you could open the door. I don't remember that Grandpa ever did show up on Christmas, but his presence was felt.

Celebrating Christmas became a custom for Lillian and me and the kids, and we used to buy gifts and hide them away in the closets and then stay up the night before wrapping them. The kids bought gifts too, and they would wrap them, and everybody would run around looking for wrapping paper and tags. In the morning the kids could go down and shake their presents, but not open any, except the ones that were in their stockings. In their stockings was always an orange, which they had to eat before the candy. We have a lot of pictures of piles of Christmas presents.

Sometimes Lillian and I would buy presents for the kids a long time before Christmas and hide them away unwrapped with the intention of wrapping them later. I recall one year, as we were digging out these presents from the backs of closets, we came upon a lovely Shirley Temple doll, about 20" long in a box. Neither of us could remember having bought it, but it had to be for Nina because she was the only one the right age. So we wrapped it and put it under the tree along with the other presents. In the morning when Nina got around to opening it, her comment was, "It's just like the one I got last year." It was indeed just like it, in fact it was it. She had never really played with it, and we had put it up in the closet to save for her. I still have it someplace - still in the same box.

# ABOUT MY BODY

I think it's appropriate to include here something about my personal physical fetishes and vices. I am one of those fortunate people who has never had to diet, and my normal consumption of food is impressive. I particularly like breakfast. It's not all luck, however. I am physically very active. I still jog a little some mornings before breakfast, and if not, I do about 10 minutes of calisthenics. For many years I rode a bike to and from work, about 12 miles a day. I play racquetball (singles) once or twice a week, and I still prefer to go up stairs two at a time. I had to cut down on my jogging because my right knee started hurting, but now that the knee is okay again, it's hard to get my wind back, and I still worry about that knee.

I take 2 or 3 grams of vitamin C a day, and have done it for about 12 years. I think it protects me from colds (and maybe from cancer). I also take a multivitamin every day.

I have a strange fetish about my hair. After a shower I rub it vigorously, 20 strokes with each palm without soap or shampoo. I think that pulls on the hair roots and keeps them healthy.

What I do about my teeth is not so unusual. About 10 years ago, after I had classic gum problems, Clement Alpert, my dentist, suggested that I brush a mixture of Hydrogen Peroxide and baking soda up into my gums. I do that almost every night after I brush my teeth and use a Water Pick on them. Recently I saw an article about Pyorrhea which said that dentists were divided into two schools of thought; periodontistry and the peroxide-baking soda approach. I'm for the latter. I've had no more gum problems since I started it, and it's a long time.

By the way, there's a story I should tell about my dentist. I asked him one day how come a nice Jewish boy, whose mother hardly spoke English, came to have a name like Clement. It seems that his birth certificate says Kalman, but when the nice

Catholic lady next door heard that his mother had a son and had named him Kalman, she said, "That's nice - we'll call him Clement." Somehow it stuck.

I'm 5 ft 10" and weigh about 152 lbs. I used to weigh 167, but I cut out drinking a lot of milk (3 glasses a day) because I think it made my nose run. The loss of weight followed that change in habits, and I concluded about 3 years ago, after Dr. Goldenberg, in an extensive and costly search, could find no other symptom, that there was a cause and effect relationship there.

I gave up cigarettes about 30 years ago, but I still smoke a pipe. I cut down on my smoking by not lighting up before noon. I honestly don't know why I keep smoking. It's a crazy habit I can do without -but ...

# MY NEPHEW'S SUICIDE ATTEMPT

About 15 years ago my family was in great turmoil because Leland, Eddie's youngest son, had tried to commit suicide. I heard it from Sylvia and then from Elaine, but there were no details. That's all his mother, Claire, had told them, and I guess one normally would not ask for details in such a situation.

I called Claire and after some condolences and comforting, I pressed her for the gory details. At first she evaded by assuring me again that he had tried to commit suicide and changing the subject, but I was suspicious and pressed on. Finally I learned that he had opened the window in his bedroom on a cold day and lain on his bed naked in an attempt to catch pneumonia.

Leland is now married and has two children. He's a computer analyst at a hospital in Connecticut.

# COIT TOWER

Colt Tower is on Telegraph Hill in San Francisco. On the ground floor the walls are painted with murals all around the circular hall which rings the elevators. The murals were done in the 30s as part of some WPA type project.

The first time I visited Coit Tower, which was probably in the 1940s, I was surprised by one particular street scene. It contained, among other people, a rich man and a worker. You could clearly identify them because the rich man wore a Chesterfield Coat and held The Wall Street Journal in one hand, while the worker wore a cap and leather jacket. The rich man had his hand in the worker's pocket. The symbolism was clear and appropriate to the 30s, although 15 years later it was notable.

About 10 years later I revisited the tower and looked for that particular scene. It was gone. There was a new figure on that mural, right in front of where I remembered the hand-in-pocket bit to have been. I went all over the tower asking people about it. Finally I found a manager type who told me that several years before they had invited all the original painters back to re-touch their work. The original artist, now successful somewhere, had added the new figure to the scene.

# FRANKLIN'S EYE

When Franklin was about 6 months old, Anna and I took him to England to visit his great grandparents. On the flight over, which was a crowded overnight flight, they provided him with a bassinette, but it was much too small for a 6 month old child. Besides that, he was terribly uncomfortable for other reasons which were not obvious to us at the time. So mostly he slept in my seat while I stood up and joined the conversation at the end of the cabin. Sometimes I sat in Anna's seat while she stood, but we spent a thoroughly uncomfortable night.

Anna's father had arranged for someone to meet us at Heathrow Airport in the morning and bring us a car, which we would use while we were there. It was an old car Aubrey owned part of. However, somehow the signals got crossed, and we were not met. The person he had arranged to bring the car thought it was a different date. All of this got straightened out after two or three phone calls and a few hours wait. Then the car arrived and we got in it and drove to Edenbridge. The plan was for us to stay at the Pryce's house there. After some problem about not having the key, we finally found someone who had it, and we entered the house. It was June, but incredibly cold, and the heat was turned off. The house had the kind of electric heat that involves storage, so you can only store heat in the heaters over night and then use it during the daytime. There was no heat stored in the heaters because it was June, so there wasn't any way of getting heat into the place. You could plug an ordinary electric heater into the wall, and in fact we did find one after a while and plugged that in, which made the upstairs bedroom just barely bearable. We were exhausted from not having slept the night before, so Franklin, Anna and I got into the bed in the upstairs bedroom very early, both from fatigue and to keep warm. Franklin seemed to have a cold and slept fitfully.

As I was dozing off, I was awakened by extremely loud music which seemed to be in the same room. The Pryce house in Edenbridge is the middle one in a row of three, and there was a party in the next house. It was not just in the next house. It seemed to me that the speakers must have been in the room adjoining our bedroom. Further, they must have been up against that wall. The party went on until 2 o'clock in the morning. The songs I remember most distinctly are one about Andy Jackson took a load of bacon and a load of beans, and a yellow submarine. Sometime after midnight Anna put in a call to the local police, which seemed to help for about half an hour or so, and then things went back the way they were. By 2 o'clock in the morning it ended and we slept.

I had a frightening thought, as one often does in a new situation, that I was seeing the Pryce house in a typical condition, i.e., that this sort of a party went on next door every night. But fortunately it didn't. The next night was quiet and we had a good sleep. In between I arranged for a baby carriage for Franklin, we explored the town, and the weather warmed up. In fact it warmed up to such an extent that within 4 days we were swimming in the ocean at Hastings.

The car was one that Aubrey owned in partnership with someone in England. It was serviceable. The only peculiarity was that the pointer, which indicated which gear you were in (forward, neutral, etc.), seemed to have broken or become detached, and it didn't work. So when you changed the lever position on the automatic transmission, you were sometimes uncertain where you were. But after a while I got the feel of it, and it was alright. Driving on the left was a continuing annoyance which would become acute at difficult times.

After that first night, it was really very pleasant. We used the house in Edenbridge as our headquarters. Onra used to call it her cottage in Kent. We visited the surrounding countryside, including Churchill's house at Chartwell, and all the other stately homes in Kent. We visited Onra's mother and father in Stapleford, and the next door neighbor didn't have another party.

After about a week, Franklin woke up one morning crying, with his left eye swung in so that the eyeball was only half showing. We managed to locate a doctor, but he couldn't see us until 5 o'clock that afternoon. He was part of a hospital group nearby. That day we were scheduled to go to Blackheath to pick up Anna's other grandmother, Grandma Pryce, and bring her for a short visit in Edenbridge. We decided to go ahead and make the trip because our schedule was tight. There was no other time we could visit Grandma Pryce, and there was nothing we could do about Franklin anyhow until 5 o'clock when we had our appointment with the doctor. He had moments when he was not crying and moments when he was.

He was really not too bad on the trip to Blackheath, although his eye stayed in the corner. On the way back though, we were late, we were lost, and he started screaming unreasonably. That was the most uncomfortable few hours I ever spent in my life; driving on the left side of the street, with a screaming child, through countryside I was unfamiliar with, mostly lost, and turning onto the wrong roads, worried about being late for a doctor's appointment. Franklin screamed all the way. When we arrived at the doctor's office and parked the car, he stopped crying. When we took him up to the doctor's office, he was smiling. The doctor looked at him and the first thing he said was, "Well, this is a happy baby."

I thought I would strangle him right then, but I restrained myself and he added, "What seems to be the problem?" I said, "Look at his eye."

He looked and said, "Well, he does have a bit of a squint." At that point the doctor took over the situation. He told us not to worry about the squint. He had a grandson who had a squint. It was just one of these things, and there wasn't very much you could do about it, and that's the way life was, and keep smiling, and keep your chin up. By the end of the discussion I wished I had strangled him at the beginning.

We only had about 2 more days to stay in England at this point, and Franklin seemed to be comfortable in the sense that he wasn't crying furiously any more, but his eye stayed locked into the corner. When we got back to the states we immediately made an appointment with the foremost eye specialist in the area, the great Dr. Parks, who lived in a magnificent mansion on Massachusetts Avenue. He had two examining rooms and two nurses, and he dictated all the while he examined. A very model of erudition.

His judgment was almost immediate. The child had Duane's Syndrome. An Immediate operation was desirable. The operation involved fixing the eye so that he couldn't move it anymore, but at least it would be forward; it would look good, and he could use it a little. Of course in some uncertain number of years the eye would atrophy from not being properly used, but it was important to do the operation immediately. This judgment was derived from a series of observations and reflex texts, which somehow also considered, but did not completely rule out the possibility that there was a brain tumor. We were supposed to be relieved that it was not likely to be a brain tumor.

Anna and I decided that we were not about to take him into the hospital immediately for that kind of an operation, and that we'd better go home and think about it. I intended to seek another opinion. When I got home I took down my copy of Cecil Loeb's Textbook of Medicine and looked up Duane's Syndrome. The first thing it said about Duane's Syndrome was that it was congenital. I recalled Anna carefully explaining to the doctor the circumstances of the inception of the problem. She called him. He assured her that she had never told him anything to indicate that the child had not had it since birth. Further, he said that he thought the child had had it since birth. That sent us scurrying for his baby pictures. We thought perhaps he might have had a little deviation of that eye, but the baby pictures were very clear. The eyes were perfect.

At about that time we began to notice that the eye didn't always stay in the corner. Sometimes it came out a little bit. It seemed to be coming out a little bit more each time. We decided to wait, and that proved to be exactly the right thing. Little by little the eye straightened itself out, although for several years we observed that when he got a cold, the left eye seemed to wander in a little bit.

That hasn't happened for at least 4 or 5 years now, and he seems to be completely recovered. So the grandfatherly English doctor, who seemed unconcerned about a bit of a squint was really the hero of the affair. I'm glad I didn't strangle him....

# C.B. BROWN

Charles Bradner Brown was sometimes called "Brad Brown, usually C.B. Brown, occasionally when he was not around, Horseface Brown, but never Charlie Brown, He was in everyone's estimation, the champion story teller at White Oak. He worked as an engineer in the oil fields in the thirties, and in his words, "I could tell you a thousand true stories about the oil fields, and some of them actually happened." I intend to tell you one of his stories, but before I do, I can't resist noting the fact that he worked for me for a few years when I headed the systems analysis group of The Undersea Warfare Research & Development Planning Council. During that time I discovered that he absolutely could not write a coherent sentence. What that means in terms of story tellers I'm not sure, but if you listen to people tell a story, you will find that they really do not talk in sentences.

This particular story of his goes back to the days when, as a fresh graduate engineer, he took a job in an oil company in which his father was the vice president. In those days jobs were pretty scarce, and if your relatives didn't make one for you, you probably didn't have one. It was never clear to him really what his job was, and he messed around with the office work and the accounts and various things, and made a great discovery. He came in to tell the president of the company about it one day. He told him that he had discovered how the company could save a great deal of money because they were overpaying for shipping their oil and chemicals. He had checked the rates, and what they were paying was at least 30% higher than they should have been paying. Further, they were getting this shipping done by a small company called Continental Shipping that nobody ever heard of, and was probably not very reliable. The bigger companies charged less.

The president told him, "Brad, you're a bright boy, I can see that, but forget all about this idea of yours. Continental Shipping is owned by me and your father and a few other executives here. So just go back and investigate something else."

C.B. Brown was a Quaker, and I once asked him what Quakers believe in. His unhesitating answer was, "Compound interest."

# FRED OGREENE

When I last heard of Fred he was President of Litton Industries, which ranks him among the most distinguished of the NOL alumni. During and right after the war he worked with Ed Trounson, John Buhler and me and none of us considered him particularly bright or outstanding in any way. We still don't, so maybe we must refer back to the quotation from Solomon or Anna Buckner.

The most extraordinary thing about Fred OGreene is that he's not Irish. He's Norwegian. His grandfather's name was Augren, and it got mangled when he came through Ellis Island as an immigrant.

# SEYMOUR

In the good old days when we lived on Riggs Road, it was in a kind of big old house set back off the road at a T intersection where Metzerrot Road came into Riggs Road or Old Colesville Road came into Powder Mill Road or Adelphi Road ended. If you came down the stem of the T and kept driving, you would go right through our living room. Nanny used to come visit us often, and she would stay for a few weeks, and sometimes Seymour would come down on the weekends, driving from New York. On one particular occasion, Seymour was expected, and Nanny was watching for him out the front window as she often did. He was always the apple of her eye.

She came away from the window once to say that she thought Seymour had just gone by. Then she went back to the window. About twenty minutes later she came in to say that she thought Seymour had just gone by again. She was going to go out and stand on the lawn. She did, and he came by a third time, saw her, and stopped. Each of these passes was at an enormous rate of speed, typical of Seymour. He thought he was driving on the stem of the T, but he was on the top of it.

Mel and Brian used to call him "Uncle Peanuts," and his visits were a great treat because he would "roughhouse" with them. This consisted mainly of his lying on the bed while they dove onto him from the headboard or footboard. What a physical beating he would take! But they loved it.

Seymour is an accountant, and he could store up sleep like a camel stores water. Many nights when we were all together yakking or playing pinochle until the small hours of the morning, he would stay up to do some accounting work after the rest of us went to bed and then get up with us all in the morning. On the other hand, particularly at the end of tax season, he has been known to sleep almost continuously for 3 days, only getting up for an occasional meal.

After Lillian died I set up a trust for Nina and Terri and made him the trustee. At times I have been a little sorry about that because he is hard to contact and touchy. At this point he still has custody of a lot of Terri's money and some of Nina's. He sends me a report on the trust and its earnings for tax purposes every year, but I can't get him to pay the income tax out of the trust. I have to pay it.

He married Helen during the war, before he went overseas; and divorced her in the 40s. Helen, as I recall, was a congenital liar. She preferred to lie even when telling the truth was easier and would do no damage. They had one child, Warren, who is now somewhere in California. Seymour doesn't talk to him. He cut him off completely when he was 13. I often wonder where Warren is and how he's making out. I liked him. We went camping with him and Seymour once at Lake George. He used to call Brian Shortie-cake.

Seymour married Mitzi in the 60s and had a girl, Jackie. Mitzi had a daughter, Pam, by an earlier marriage, and Seymour adopted her. They are now divorced, and Seymour broke contact with Mitzi and the two children. He now lives in New Mexico and is married to his former secretary, Mildred (Mitzi's real name was also Mildred). That marriage seems okay. Mildred, as his secretary, always looked after him better than either of his wives anyhow. She reminded him to visit his mother and kept track of birthdays, etc. She's a good friend of my cousin Helen and I like her. I hope they make it together.

# PEOPLE LOOK FAMILIAR IN NEW YORK

After Lillian and I had lived in Washington for several years, I think it was about the time Melvin was born, I took a 6 week summer course at Columbia University, mostly so that we would have the advantage of staying with the Buckners, who had taken a cottage in Far Rockaway. Far Rockaway has a magnificent beach. It was a kind of hectic six weeks for me because I had to travel into New York every day on the subway. The worst of it was that the cottage was inhabited not only by the Buckners and the Raffs, but the Plaves were also there (Rosalind, George & Diane). They would sit up and talk loudly till all hours of the night. While this was going on I could neither study nor sleep, and it was rather exasperating.

However, the thing which sticks in my mind was the day Lillian and I were walking along the Rockaway beach, and I made the observation to her that people seemed to look familiar here in New York, as contrasted to Washington. Maybe there were more Jewish people; maybe they just looked like people we knew. Then I said, "They just look like people we know. For instance, that tall fellow over there looks like my cousin Larry." I had picked him at random, just looking around for someone to prove my point, and then decided who he looked like. He did indeed look like my cousin Larry. Identical. It was my cousin Larry. Selma's husband, Larry Essensen. (Selma is the daughter of Aunt Jeanette, my father' sister). We stopped to talk. Selma was there, and so were several other members of the family, and we had a sort of a reunion that afternoon on the beach & for the next few days. Larry was a surgeon and they lived in Peter Cooper Apartments in downtown N.Y. He is now dead & Selma still lives there.

# THE BUDGET

Shortly after Lillian and I were married there was a period when we went on a budget. She had envelopes in which she would put dollar bills and change that we needed for the phone bill, the laundry, for food, and for various other things. There must have been about a dozen envelopes which she stuffed every time we got paid. On each envelope there was written an amount of money which we were supposed to put in it each week. Of course, some weeks we would need a little more money for some things and a little less for others, so she would never put in exactly the amount of money it said on each envelope. We went along this way for about a year, until one day I had the temerity to add up the amounts written on all the envelopes. They added up to more money than we made in a week. We had been doing this for a long time without discovering that fact. It was a bit of a shock, and ever since then I have set very little store by budgets.

# MY HUSBAND WILL NEVER BELIEVE ME

Shortly after World War II I had a rather trivial automobile accident. It had begun to snow and the snow was covering the ground very lightly, but it was incredibly slippery, and I was not aware of it. I was heading toward a red light. There was a car stopped at the light, and I realized I could not stop in time. I wasn't going very fast, but I decided the only thing to do was to hit it squarely. Perhaps that would do the least damage. I did, in fact, hit it squarely, rode over the bumper, and put a moderate dent in the trunk of the car. A woman was driving, and she got out in a sort of a panic. I said, "Don't worry about it. It's all my fault. I'll pay for the damages." She said, "My husband will never believe me."

I couldn't see any point to this statement because I admitted it was my fault, but she was distraught. I told her I would call her husband that evening and assure him that it was my fault. I did, but he was very hard to assure. He said, "You're being very gallant about this thing, but I'm sure my wife was at fault."

I said, "No. She didn't do anything wrong. It was just snowing, and I couldn't stop, and I hit her."

He said, "She stopped without signaling, didn't she?" I thought a moment and said, "You don't have to signal when you stop for a red light. Besides she was standing there for a long time before I hit her." The discussion went on for quite a while in this vain before I finally persuaded him that it was my fault. Boy! Did his wife know him! I wonder how long that marriage lasted.

# MYRON JOSEPH

There are 5 of us who have been together since high school days. We were all members of the Alpha Phi Pi fraternity, and though we've lost track of most of the other members twenty or thirty years ago, the five of us still see each other pretty often, with our wives. These are Julie, me, Myron Joseph, Al Post and Eddie Goldstone. This story is little bits and pieces that I remember about Myron Joseph.

"Jo" was the first of us to get married, and the story of his courtship has a peculiar twist to it. He dated Elizabeth for at least several years, and I'm sure they used to neck furiously. Elizabeth had a cousin named Flo who was the same age, and with whom she was very close. In fact their families lived in the same two family house, one on one floor, and the other on another. As I understand it, the entrance to the house was really the entrance for both of them, and when you rang the bell downstairs, one or the other would answer it. So it was really like two apartments, but they weren't actually separated.

Elizabeth had soft eyes. I recall that Leah is mentioned in the Bible as having soft eyes. She was Jacob's first wife. At any rate, during the years that Jo was dating Elizabeth, he was always looking for dates for Flo. The other 4 of us were single then, and we often got tapped to take Flo along. Well, one day Jo dropped Elizabeth and came to call on Flo. I find it hard to imagine that he would have the courage to walk up to that door, ring the bell and ask for Flo instead of Elizabeth, but he did; and he married Flo.

I got a call from Jo on his wedding night. He had a problem. Apparently he was so worried about Flo getting pregnant that he was using two condoms, one over the other, and they were breaking. I told him one was enough, and try a little Vaseline on it. Afterwards I thought of how strange it was that he should call me because I wasn't married, but I guess he knew something. The irony of the two condom story is that they didn't have any children when they wanted them. They went through fertility tests and the doctor told him that his sperm was somehow defective. They adopted a child, and a few years after that, they had their own.

Jo and I are the only PhDs among the 5. He was Professor of Labor Relations at Carnegie Mellon for many years. Now he is retired, doing labor arbitration exclusively. He is a person I really enjoy talking to about philosophic, economic or political subjects. He is really a very deep thinker. He also is very good with children of all ages. He understands them and has a rapport with them which may come from his educational experience, although I think it's deeper than that. He once got an award from Carnegie-Mellon for excellence in teaching, which I consider a marvelous compliment in a world where, at Universities, it's only research that counts.

In his later years he has taken up magic as a hobby; slight of hand and things like that. He's really very good at it. He's just the kind of guy you'd expect to come up with an interesting hobby like that later in life.

I remember that his father's name is Ben, and his mother once said to a bride at a wedding, "I can only wish that you're as happy as Ben and I have been." I remember that because I consider it an absolutely awful thing to say. First of all, it's a kind of a brag disguised as good wishes. Second of all, nobody really thinks they have been that happy. Surely she must be aware of the frictions between her and Ben, which I'm sure there are. I have heard similar statements in similar circumstances, and it always revolts me.

There are many people in the world who appear to be very moral. In most cases they appear so because they want to appear so, and they are successful in their objectives. Among all the people I know, however, I would bet on Jo as being truly moral.

# HOME IMPROVEMENTS

The first major improvement at 8501 Aragon Lane was the addition of the den, which I later called the Ag Room. Ag is short for aggravation. It had been a porch which we finished in and made a room out of. The job was done by a contractor named Doyle Pendergraft.

He had a crew out, and they started with the brick work and the stone work. They started to do the stone work in a way that he termed "the right way," but Lillian stopped him right away and told him that she didn't want it "the right way;" she wanted it to match the other stone work on the front of the house. Under her tutelage he did just that, and the brick work was apparently also alright. I paid him one third before he started, and I was supposed to pay a second third when he finished enclosing the room. I gave that to him in advance because he needed the money, but the room was not finished; in particular, the door was not in place, nor was the window. The problem with the front window, he said, was that he could not get a steel casement window to match the ones that were in the house. His crew came out every day, but they had nothing to do because the next step was the windows.

Finally, in desperation, I made a call to see if I could locate the windows, and the first place I called had them. This was strange because it was one of the largest window companies in the area, and one that would naturally be called first. I put this together with certain grumblings from his workers that they hadn't been paid and concluded that he was probably going broke, and couldn't get the windows because he couldn't pay for them. I had them sent out and I paid for them. His workers were eager to get on with it, and they put in the windows, particularly the front window, which was about 4 1/2 ft high and nine feet wide. I then called a glazier from The Yellow Pages and had him glaze the window. By this time I was convinced by other events that Pendergraft was going broke and had also been passing bad checks.

The hardware had not been put in the windows, and they were held in place by bricks on the window sill. That night was windy, and I became concerned that the windows might push the bricks off the sill. I decided to put the hardware in, at least enough of it to hold the windows closed.

After considerable fumbling around with the hardware and the windows, and not getting anything to fit into place, I stood back and made the startling discovery that the whole casement was upside down. The winders to open and close the casements were at the top.

That was a sleepless night for me. The wind was blowing and noisy, and I was troubled that I had paid almost full price for a job that was not nearly completed and badly botched besides. Surely they had done lots of other less obvious things wrong. In the morning when the crew came out I announced to them that we were going to take the window out, with the glass in it, turn it upside down, and put it back. We were going to have two men on scaffolding outside and two men inside. Pendergraft showed up in the middle of the ensuing discussion, and I went over it again. He assured me that it was not feasible, and he could not be responsible if all the glass broke.

At this point I began to see some humor in the situation. He certainly was not going to be responsible. We did it, however, with no problems. The window was easy to remove. It was not properly fastened, but the entire nine foot frame was only held in with putty.

After that the work proceeded at a snail's pace, and a few days later, I believe it was a Saturday at noon, he came to me for the rest of the money. The problem was that the crew wanted to go out for lunch, and they had no money. It was payday for them, and he couldn't pay them. So would I please advance some money. They were almost finished with the outside anyhow, and the mortar work which was still to be done was prepared to the extent that the mortar was already mixed in the wheelbarrow, and they would surely finish it that afternoon. I had almost no alternative but to advance him some more money. The crew went off for lunch, and that was the last I saw of any of them. The mortar hardened in the wheelbarrow, and I buried it in the yard; not the wheelbarrow, just the big clump of mortar which I managed to get out of the barrow.

I finished it by myself, particularly the inside, where I discovered that the furring strips which had been put up to hold the paneling were not put up correctly, and there were a lot of places where one had to nail paneling with nothing to nail to. I also had to hang the outside door. I finished the interior myself, and it was a lot of work, but I got a lot of satisfaction out of it too.

A number of years later we decided to add another floor to that house. By then my memory had dimmed about the aggravation room, and I was ready to go again. Besides, at that time my company was doing well, and I was feeling rather affluent. I couldn't get anybody to give me a bid on the job, so we did it by the hour.

I have a number of little comic vignette memories from that construction. The first was when they had the outside framed in, the roof was on, but none of the ceiling joists were in place. The weight of the roof was obviously pushing the wall out. It was my custom during the construction work, which went on for many months, to come home a little early while the workers were still there, and check on what they had been doing. On this occasion, I took a level, laid it against the wall and found, as I expected, that the wall was leaning out. I called the foreman's attention to it. He said, "Impossible. They just checked it very carefully."

I said, "Well it's leaning out now." Somehow they got that fixed. The sheetrock (plasterboard) was put up by a team of three blacks who I found someplace in the classified advertising. They claimed to be a master mechanic and two helpers, but beyond a doubt, none of them had ever put sheetrock up before. The general problem with the construction was that it was the peak of a building boom, and it was very hard to get anybody experienced to work for you. I spent a lot of time with those three blacks, teaching them how to put up sheetrock. The vignette I recall was explaining to them that when you leave an opening for an electrical outlet, you can't just bash a hole in the sheetrock with a hammer, you have to carefully cut a space that the outlet will fit through. I was explaining that to them in a room filled with large sheets of sheetrock which they had not piled up neatly, but had just thrown in. One of them was standing on a sheet, and it cracked beneath his feet during my demonstration of how you cut sheetrock with a knife instead of a saw.

The master mechanic was the expert, and really did know something, the value of which I hardly understood, but he kept reminding the people working for him that before you drove a nail, you had to set the head down on the floor and bump the point with a hammer. He was firmly convinced that doing this was the essence of being a good mechanic.

The floors were a particular problem because we couldn't get anybody who really knew how to lay a hardwood floor. That has to be done right, or it creaks forever. We therefore decided on plywood floors, to be covered with carpet. However, somehow it was 3/8" plywood, which does not make a sturdy floor, and feels kind of scary when you walk on it. After it was in, I decided that the thing to do was to put another layer of plywood on top. I came home to inspect the work that night and found that the carpenters were very carefully putting the second floor over the first so that all the joints lined up.

The other problem with the floor was that one day while they were nailing down the second layer of plywood; Lillian called to tell me that the refrigerator had stopped working. I didn't worry about it too much, but when I got home that evening I discovered that a fuse had blown. I replaced it and it blew again. Obviously one of the nails in that floor had gone into an electrical wire. By this point there was already one layer of plywood over the entire floor, and a second layer over two thirds of it. Bill Dunham, who worked for Raff Associates at the time and was also involved in building, came out that night to help me check the place over. I discussed that problem with him. He had a brilliant idea which worked. We took an ohmmeter and ran one wire to the shorted socket. With the other one we went around touching nail heads until the meter showed a short. We pulled that nail, and under it was found the pierced BX cable. We cut out a section of the floor, and repaired the cable.

The whole series of comic episodes started with an architect from Clotille-Smith, a rather large and expensive architectural firm in the Washington area. He made the initial designs, which we had to throw away because he really didn't know anything about architecture. The idea of putting a little "L" on a bedroom so that the door opens into the bedroom; into a little alcove, rather than bringing the hall all the way down so that the room is square; was completely unknown to him. He also didn't know the building code, and if we had built by his plans, it never would have passed inspection because the ceilings were too low. He also had the crazy idea of putting balconies outside the bedrooms, which was clearly not compatible with the size of the installation and the space available.

The last little vignette is the carpenter who was moving the basement staircase so that it would be under the upstairs staircase. He spent three days leveling the supporting wall and the top step because he was afraid to cut the joists. He had some kind of a vision of the house falling down when he cut the joists to let the staircase go through. When I recognized his psychological problem, I took his skill saw and cut all the necessary joists while he watched. He was amazed that nothing moved.

At any rate, it was all finished, it was comfortable, we enjoyed it for many years, and we proved the truth of Ralph Drosd's quotation.

# ORANGE JUICE AND
# PULP AND THINGS LIKE THAT

When I was in college I used to work nights for The Bronx Home News, which was a newspaper on 138th St. in The Bronx. I was in the classified advertising department, and I used to take want-ads, 5 to 9 on weekdays, 9 to 1 on Saturday, and every other Sunday, 6 to 9 PM.

There were all kinds of rules about taking want ads. Some had to do with credit. Some had to do with the wording of ads; there could not be any hint that a man was going to share an apartment with a woman. Situation wanted ads had to be paid for in advance. Job opportunities had to be confirmed. All death notices had to be read back to the undertaker on a separate call after you checked the undertaker's phone number, and a hundred other rules of that type. Every evening when I came in at 5 o'clock, the assistant manager, Joe Gallagher would be sitting at his desk at the back of the large classified advertising office where we all worked. There would be a stack of yellow sheets of paper on the far right corner of his desk. These were my mistakes from the night before. We would have a little routine where he would turn them over one at a time, point out each mistake, and say to me, "Now I think you must have known about that," or "This is a mistake you've made several times before."

Coming to work for the first few months was a very painful experience. After I became more at ease with things and could handle my job better, I realized what the problem had been. It was that the other man who worked with me, Joe Tepperman, was almost as new as I was, and wasn't catching any of my mistakes, which he should have been, right on the spot. He was the "night manager," and got about 2 dollars more a week for checking my copy.

This story, however, has to do with a time, about 2 years later, when the Newspaper Guild was attempting to organize the advertising employees of The Bronx Home News. There was an independent union organized too, and an NLRB election was held to select which of the two would represent us. The independent union won by one vote. It was helped by a series of frightening articles written by Westbrook Pegler about communism in the newspaper guild. After the election we discovered the following facts about the independent union: all power to negotiate with the company was vested in the board of directors; the board of directors had already been elected to serve for a period of 5 years; the President of the union was the nephew of the man who owned the newspaper.

Many years later, when Lillian and I lived on Riggs Road in Prince Georges County, there was a lot of concern among the citizenry about corruption in The Prince Georges County government. A coalition of citizens associations was formed to organize a reform party which would put candidates up for election to county offices, and presumably throw the rascals out. To organize this independent reform party, a big meeting was held with perhaps 500 or more people there from the various civic associations. Their first action was to elect a board of directors for this reform party. The board would select candidates for the new party and do publicity and solicit funds and all of that. People got up and made speeches nominating other people to the board of directors, and votes were taken, and everything was going very well until one elderly gentleman, Mr. Mulligan, who had been a member of the Prince Georges County machine and was now very active in the citizen's association, went around the hall to locate the various heads of the local citizens associations to inform them that the people being nominated and elected to the board were closely affiliated in one way or another with the Prince Georges County political machine. By the time the word got around, the 5 man board had been elected, and they all belonged to the political machine that we were trying to throw out. We tried to straighten it out, once the word got around, by increasing the board to 11 members, and using the presidents of the local civic associations in caucus to decide who were legitimate candidates, but the reform movement never amounted to much. I think we really lost the bubble at that first meeting.

I recently discovered that the frozen orange juice industry in Florida doesn't waste anything. The orange peels are used for cattle fodder and the pulp is sold to the people who make artificial orange juice.

The moral of these three stories put together is something like, "Don't ever underestimate the deviousness of entrepreneurial types."

# A POEM I WROTE TO BOB FROSCH ON HIS 40TH BIRTHDAY

Welcome to the wonderful forties
It's the prime and the harvest of life
In his forties a man's in command of his world,
With one likely exception: his wife.

A man gets a certain patina
From life and its sorrows and joy
He acquires savoir faire and a calm joie de vivre,
And likely some avoir du pois.

In his forties a man is magnetic
With the girls he's both witty and sage
He's Pasteur, JFK, Monte Cristo and Freud,
Though mostly to girls of his age.

Oh the virtues of forty summers
Are so clear and so brightly they shine
That the wise always yearn to be forty...of course,
To be wise one must pass thirty-nine.

# DIET BOOK

I am a physicist, and not a physician. So what can you learn about dieting from a physicist? Well, ever since the apple fell on Sir Isaac Newton, physicists have known a lot about weight. For one thing, did you know that there are 8 negative calories in a glass of ice water?

That's right -- negative calories. That's not a trick or a joke. When you drink a glass of cold water, you use up 8 calories of food or fat, or whatever.

A calorie is an amount of energy, like kilowatt hours or foot pounds. Now there is a law of nature called the conservation of energy, which says that energy can't be created or destroyed, but only changed from one form to another. So chemical energy, which you take in in the form of food, can be changed into heat energy, just like you burn a log to get heat. The log got its energy, of course, from the sun, and stored it as chemical energy, mostly lignites and wood fiber, until you burned it -- then out it came. Your body takes in chemical energy from food. Only green plants can take energy from the sun and store it. Your body stores this energy as fat; at least if there's too much of it. It can store some of it as sugar in your blood, and use some of it to make muscle and other body parts, and to keep itself warm, and walk up stairs, and things like that. If, however, there is too much energy, it makes fat, and that's what we're up against.

Now after you drink that glass of cold water, you have to get rid of it. But it comes out warm. Since energy is conserved, and heat is energy, where did your body get the energy to warm that water? It must have come from the food you ate, either directly or from some of the chemical energy your body has stored in it, hopefully as fat. It's not hard for a physicist to show that the amount of energy required to warm that ice water to body temperature is about 8 calories. A calorie (to a physicist it is really a large calorie, or a kilocalorie) is the amount of heat required to raise the temperature of a liter of water one degree centigrade. So there you are! That energy came from your food.

Before you rush to the sink and the ice cube tray however, let me point out that there are about 2000 calories in a pound of fat, and a little arithmetic shows that amounting to 250 glasses of ice water, a prodigious quantity to pass through your kidneys. At 2 glasses per hour, 16 hours a day, it would take 8 days, and ruin your kidneys.

# THE KING AND THE CABBAGE SOUP, A STORY MY MOTHER LIKED TO TELL

One morning a king was out hunting and became separated from his retinue and lost in the woods. He wandered all day until after nightfall he found a woodcutter's hut. He knocked on the door and was recognized. The woodcutter and his wife humbly invited him to share their supper. It was cabbage soup. The king had never tasted cabbage soup before, and it was delicious. Early in the morning the woodcutter showed the king the way back to his castle.

That night the king called his cook. "How come we never have cabbage soup?" he asked.

"That's peasant food," the cook replied. "Kings eat much better food."

"Well I want cabbage soup," the king insisted. "Make it for dinner tomorrow!"

The next night the king had cabbage soup, but it didn't taste nearly as good as what the woodcutter's wife had made. He fired the cook and got a new one.

He asked the new cook for cabbage soup, and he got it, but again it was nothing like the delicious soup he remembered eating in the woodcutter's cottage. He decided to make the woodcutter's wife his royal cook, and he sent for her.

When she came and heard the story she said, "Your majesty, have you ever in your life been so long without eating as the night you came to our cottage?"

He had to admit that he could not remember another time, and she said, "All the spices and the best cooking in the world cannot take the place of hunger."

Printed in the United States
107386LV00001B/28/A